THE ULTIMATE
AIR FRYER OVEN
COOKBOOK

THE ULTIMATE
AIR FRYER OVEN
COOKBOOK

EASY RECIPES THAT SATISFY

Coco Morante

Photography by Katie Newburn

MARINER BOOKS
An Imprint of HarperCollinsPublishers
Boston   New York

Photography © 2021 by Katie Newburn
Food styling by Nathan Carrabba
Prop styling by Katie Newburn and Nathan Carrabba

INSTANT® and associated logos are owned by Instant Brands Inc. and are used
under license.

marinerbooks.com

Book design by Melissa Lotfy

Library of Congress Cataloging-in-Publication Data has been applied for.
ISBN 978-0-358-65012-6 (hbk)
ISBN 978-0-358-64992-2 (ebk)

Printed in the United States of America
1 2021
4500828518

To Eve,
my favorite kitchen helper
and taste tester

CONTENTS

CHAPTER 1

BREAKFAST & BRUNCH

CHAPTER 9

PANTRY

INTRODUCTION

There are air fryers, and then there are air fryer *ovens.* With their ample cooking space, powerful convection, and top and bottom heating elements, these appliances are so much more versatile than their predecessors. They represent a huge upgrade from either a basket-style air fryer or a basic toaster oven, with so much more power and versatility.

Instant Brands sells a wide variety of air frying appliances. This cookbook is focused specifically on the biggest and best of the bunch—the air fryer ovens in the Omni line. They come in both 18- and 26-liter sizes, with the names Omni, Omni Plus, and Omni Pro. From here on out we'll refer to them as Omni ovens. The recipes in this book will work without modification in any model of either size. If you have an air fryer oven appliance from another brand, similar cooking times, temperatures, and cooking programs can be used, but you may find that some slight adjustments are necessary.

The Omni ovens have a wide variety of cooking programs, designed to help you easily select the time, temperature, and convection level suited to whatever food you are preparing. The selection of cooking programs differs slightly on the two sizes of ovens, but there are no tasks that can't be done in either one. For instance, the 26-liter Omni Plus has a **SLOW COOK** program, but with the right timing and temperature settings, you can use the **BAKE** program on the 18-liter Omni Plus to accomplish the same ends. Whenever this is the case in a recipe, both options will be listed.

Because these ovens are so versatile, the recipes and methods in this book run the gamut: You'll learn how to use your air fryer oven not only to air fry, but also to roast, rotisserie, bake, broil, slow cook, and dehydrate, and even to proof dough. My recipes are clearly written and easy to follow step by step, and I'll often give flavor variations as well as basic instructions for more pared-down versions. For instance, you can cook up a pan of praline-coated bacon or just plain bacon—there are instructions for both. Whether you want to whip up homemade latkes or simply heat up a batch of frozen Tater Tots, you'll find recipes here.

I made sure to incorporate lots of different breadings, coatings, spice mixtures, and sauces in this cookbook so that cooking through it will teach you many ways to prepare your favorite crispy and flavorful "fried" foods. The Pantry chapter contains homemade condiments and other basics that will take your cooking up a level, but you can also substitute in store-bought items if you would like to keep things simple. It's all up to you.

I hope that you enjoy cooking in your Omni oven as much as I do in mine. This appliance has truly revolutionized the way I get meals on the table. Whether it's roasted zucchini and carrots in under 20 minutes (page 220), fresh "bagels" for a weekend morning treat (page 53), or a beautifully burnished Basque-style cheese-cake (page 247) to impress and delight dinner guests, you really can do it all in this amazing countertop oven.

The following introductory pages will walk you through using all of the functions of your appliance. I'll tell you about my favorite accessories and tools to use with the air fryer oven, most of which you're likely to have in your kitchen already. I'll also talk about air fryer pantry staples, give you my best tips for air fryer oven care and cleaning, and list some helpful FAQs. Let's get cooking.

COCO MORANTE

HOW TO USE THE AIR FRYER OVEN

Air fryer ovens are very intuitive machines to use. If you've ever operated a toaster oven, you won't find there's much of a steep learning curve as far as operating the appliance goes. However, there are some important things to know, which we'll go over here.

First off, it's a good idea to open the manual that comes with your appliance and become acquainted with all of the different programmed settings. Different air fryers have different cooking programs and accessories included, and you'll want to be able to take advantage of them all.

Most air fryer ovens will, at the very least, come with an air frying basket, a wire oven rack, and a cooking pan. The Omni ovens also come with a rotisserie spit. With all of these accessories, you'll be able to do so much more than air frying. (In the coming pages, I'll also talk about my other favorite accessories and tools to use with the air fryer oven, most of which you're likely to have in your kitchen already.)

Omni ovens currently come in two different sizes: 18 liters (a little over 4 gallons) and 26 liters (a little under 6 gallons). Though it might seem like this would make a big difference in capacity, it actually doesn't—the extra liters are mostly in height rather than width or depth of the cooking space. So you'll be able to fit most of the same cookware in both sizes of air fryer oven. More than size, choosing between these machines really comes down to what you like in terms of aesthetics, safety features, and price point.

Preheating, Cooking, and Keep Warm

While some basket-style air fryers begin cooking right when you press the "**Start**" button, air fryer ovens generally have a short preheating cycle on most of their cooking programs. Happily, this takes much less time than preheating a traditional oven. The Omni ovens take 2 to 4 minutes to preheat, depending on the cooking temperature. The cooking status indicator at the top of the display will change from "**preheating**" to "**cooking**" when the oven has preheated, and the oven will beep as well. For best results, wait until your air fryer oven has

preheated to cook the food when the cooking program requires it, unless a recipe instructs otherwise.

Some cooking programs, such as **TOAST**, **SLOW COOK**, **REHEAT**, and **DEHYDRATE**, do not have a preheating cycle. With those programs, you'll put the food in the cold oven, then select the cooking program and press "**Start**" for the cooking program to begin. The cooking status indicator will read "**cooking**" from the start of the program.

There is also a "**keep warm**" cooking status indicator on all of the Omni ovens. The "**keep warm**" status indicator turns on at the end of the **AIR FRY**, **BAKE**, **ROAST**, and **BROIL** cooking programs and switches to "**off**" once the oven cools down to 180°F.

High and Low Convection

Most of the cooking programs on the Omni ovens can be set to either high or low convection. This allows you to change the speed of the convection fan. On the "**hi**" setting, the airflow is quite strong, to the point that lighter items will be blown around, including any parchment paper or aluminum foil that is not being held down by somewhat heavy food items. You would not, for instance, want to cook s'mores on the high convection setting.

Unless a specific setting is indicated in a recipe, leave the oven on its default "**lo**" setting.

There are a few cooking programs that cannot toggle between low and high convection: **AIR FRY**, **WARM**, and **TOAST**. When the **AIR FRY** program is running, the fan is always on high convection. When the **WARM** program is on, the fan is always set to low convection. The **TOAST** program does not have a "**hi**" or "**lo**" convection setting.

Turn Food

Omni ovens have a unique and useful feature: When it is time to flip, stir, or rotate the food, as suggested in a given recipe, it will beep and show a status message that reads "**turn food**." This message comes on two-thirds of the way through the cooking time in the **AIR FRY** and **BAKE** programs, as well as in the **ROAST** program when the rotisserie is turned off. You do not have to press any buttons to turn on this feature; in the cooking programs listed, it will automatically come on. I will sometimes set a phone timer as well, though, especially if I am leaving the room and might not hear the oven beep.

While you are not required to turn the food during the cooking process, it does ensure that foods will be evenly browned and crisped. However, if a recipe does not instruct you to turn the food when the "**turn food**" message appears, you can ignore it. The oven will continue its cooking program uninterrupted.

COOKING PROGRAMS and PRESETS

Each air fryer oven has a slightly different selection of cooking programs, and each cooking program has a defined range of temperatures, cooking times, and convection settings. However, you don't need to feel completely locked in to using the "correct" program for whatever you are making. They are mostly there to help you quickly zero in on the best settings for a given recipe. We'll talk about all of them here.

Air Fry

This is the program you'll use for any recipes that are made in the air frying basket. Think breaded items such as chicken tenders (page 179) and mozzarella sticks (page 94), foods you'd like to crisp evenly on all sides such as chickpeas (page 129) and Brussels sprouts (page 213), and meats that benefit from having their fat render and drip away, such as hamburgers (page 145) and steaks (page 137). (It might seem like an extra fuss to cook meats in the air frying basket rather than on the cooking pan, but you do actually save a lot in cleanup,

since the air directs most of the spatter down into the cooking pan this way rather than onto the sides of the oven.)

Only the top heating elements and heating coil are turned on while the **AIR FRY** program is on, similar to how a basket-style air fryer operates. The Omni oven's air frying basket sits directly on the wire oven rack when air frying to allow airflow all around the food in the basket. To avoid extra mess and cleanup, always remember to place the black enamel cooking pan in the lowest position of the oven, above the bottom heating elements, to act as a drip tray. This way, you'll catch any crumbs or grease, and the bottom heating elements will remain clean.

On the Omni ovens, the **AIR FRY** program has a temperature range of 180°F to 450°F and a cooking time range of 1 minute to 45 minutes.

Toast

A self-explanatory program, you'll select **TOAST** to make, well, toast. It's also great for warming flatbreads, bagels, and other breads straight from the freezer. This program does not have a preheat cycle—just like when you're using any other toaster, the cooking begins right when you press "**Start**." On the Omni ovens, rather than adjusting this program to a specific time and temperature, you are able to select the number of slices and the level of browning you prefer, and the oven adjusts the heat and time accordingly. You'll place breads directly on the wire oven rack when using this program. Make sure the cooking pan is not in the oven, as it will block the heat from the bottom heating elements, causing uneven toasting. (Oh, and if you notice that the toasting time varies from one use to the next, that's likely because the oven has adjusted to account for still being warm.)

Bake

Yes, you can make wonderful cakes (page 250), cookies (page 255), and brownies (page 264) in your air fryer oven. All of the Omni ovens are big enough to comfortably fit most Pyrex, ceramic, and metal baking dishes and pans. The one exception would be a typical handled glass or ceramic 9×13-inch casserole dish. In this size, you'll need to find one without handles (the metal ones from USA PAN fit nicely). On the opposite end of the size spectrum, I love using the Pyrex Littles baking dishes for smaller recipes, like poached shrimp (page 195).

Bake directly on the black enamel cooking pan that comes with your Omni oven or, when using a baking dish or pan in the Omni oven, stack it on top of the cooking pan rather than on the wire oven rack. The cooking pan fits more snugly in the rack positions than the wire rack, so heavier dishes will not cause it to fall out of place as the wire rack might. (The wire rack is better suited to lighter items such as toast or anything you are preparing in the air frying basket.)

Both the bottom and top heating elements heat up on the **BAKE** program, so the air fryer oven works like a traditional oven, except it's much faster and more efficient. After a fast preheating cycle, the oven beeps and the cooking program begins, counting down from the specified cooking time. Once you've been using your air fryer oven for a while, you'll get a sense of when you need to turn it on, as it preheats so fast and you'll want to be ready to put the food in when the countdown starts. (If you preheat the oven too soon, though, you can always re-enter the proper cooking time once you put in the food.)

The **BAKE** program can be used for more than baked goods. Baked fish, a casserole, a cooking pan full of vegetables . . . they can all be cooked with this program with great results.

Broil

Similar to a traditional oven, the air fryer oven's **BROIL** program makes use of the heating elements and heating coil at the top of the oven and starts right away, without a preheating cycle. The highest rack position is labeled for broiling use, but I often will broil foods one notch down, in the second-highest position designated for the air frying basket. (You can place the cooking pan, wire oven rack, or air frying basket on any position you choose, but if you're broiling something that's tall or in a high-sided baking dish, the highest position is often a little too close to the heat.)

Roast/Rotisserie

Select the **ROAST** program on the Omni ovens for any foods you'd roast on a sheet pan (meats, vegetables, etc.). Use the black enamel cooking pan alone or with another baking pan or baking dish on top. Roasting has two modes of use, depending on whether or not the "**Rotate**" function is engaged. Having "**Rotate**" on is the default when you are using the **ROAST** program—you'll need to press "**Rotate**" to turn it off. When the "**Rotate**" function is on, the **ROAST** program works as a rotisserie. Only the top heating elements and heating coil are on, and the food will rotate on the rotisserie spit. When the "**Rotate**" function is off, the **ROAST** program works exactly like the **BAKE** program, with both the top and bottom heating elements in use.

When I use the **ROAST** program with the rotisserie spit and the "**Rotate**" function engaged, I like to put the cooking pan on the lowest rack position, underneath the rotisserie spit, to catch any dripping grease. It's also a convenient way to cook something else on the cooking pan at the same time, like potatoes with a pork tender-

loin roast (page 154). This is fine to do, since the bottom heating elements are not turned on.

If the food needs a little more clearance on the bottom to rotate properly, though, you can use the rotisserie function without the cooking pan underneath. When doing this, many people line the bottom crumb tray with foil for easier cleanup, but this is not recommended by Instant Brands.

Slow Cook

This program works similarly to the "low" setting on a crock-style slow cooker or Instant Pot. It heats to a mellow cooking temperature of 210°F, perfect for tender, fall-apart chicken breasts (page 185) and even desserts like ultra-fudgy brownies (page 264). You can use the cooking pan or any baking dish to slow cook foods. I like the convenience of cooking and serving out of an 8-inch square Pyrex baking dish, which fits perfectly in all of the Omni ovens. For meats or other foods that you don't want to dry out, cover the baking dish with foil or any other heat-safe cover.

If your Omni oven does not come with a **SLOW COOK** program, you can accomplish the same thing by using the **BAKE** program at 210°F. You will be limited by the time range of the **BAKE** program, as it maxes out at 4 hours, rather than 20 hours on the **SLOW COOK** program. This has not been an issue for me—all of the slow-cooked recipes in this book have cooking times of just 2 hours.

Reheat

The **REHEAT** program operates within a lower temperature range and shorter cooking time range than the **ROAST** and **BAKE** programs, as it is meant for reheating already cooked foods. You can easily reheat leftovers as long as they're on or in oven-safe cookware. The default time and temperature for the **REHEAT** program is 10 minutes at 300°F, sufficient for reheating most thin air-fried items such as fries and chicken tenders. For thicker items, you may want to select a lower temperature and/or longer reheating time.

Proof

If you are already an avid baker, you know that most yeasted doughs require some time to proof, or rise, before baking. There is an optimum temperature range for proofing, 70°F to 100°F. Below this range, baked goods will take a long time to rise; above this range, yeast can begin to die off due to the heat. The **PROOF** program operates within this range, with a time range of 1 minute to 4 hours. Select a lower temperature for a slower rise or a higher temperature for a faster rise. I like to cover my bowl of dough on the **PROOF** program, since the convection action can tend to dry out the top of the dough if it is left uncovered.

If your oven does not have a **PROOF** program, simply use its **DEHYDRATE** program for similar results. Just make sure you set the temperature to 100°F or lower for a successful rise.

Dehydrate

Apple chips (page 99), beef jerky (page 100), and other dehydrated foods are easy to prepare in the Omni ovens with the **DEHYDRATE** program. The air frying basket is the best tool for this program, as it allows airflow all around the food for even drying. If you like, you can also buy wire mesh stacked dehydrator racks from cookware stores or online. This will allow you to increase the dehydrating capacity of your oven considerably—helpful if you want to make larger batches.

All of the recipes in this book that make use of the **DEHYDRATE** program are designed to fit in the air frying basket that comes with the oven, but they can easily be scaled up if you use a separate dehydrating rack. The cooking times should remain the same, as long as you still have good airflow between all of the layers, though you may need to rotate the air frying basket and racks halfway through cooking for the most even results.

Warm

There is a dedicated **WARM** program on some Omni ovens. It operates in a slightly narrower temperature range than the **REHEAT** program and only makes use of the bottom heating elements for gentle warming rather than cooking. It is meant to keep already cooked food warm, without it overcooking or drying out on top. You can set it to run for up to 2 hours.

Presets

In addition to the cooking programs listed above, some models of Omni ovens have presets as well. Presets are just slightly more targeted time and temperature ranges designed for specific foods. For instance, the Omni Plus 26-liter oven has eight presets within the **AIR FRY** program, including "Fries," "Chicken," and "Veggies"; in the **REHEAT** program, there is a specific preset for pizza. To learn more about these presets, look in the Smart Programs section of your Omni oven's user manual for a chart detailing their time and temperature ranges.

The recipes in this book do not require you to select presets for individual foods but rather give specific temperature and time recommendations. This way, they can be used in any Omni oven.

MUST-HAVE TOOLS and ACCESSORIES

Here is a list of my top favorite tools and accessories to use with an air fryer oven. Of course, you can get cooking without buying any extras, but I do find that these items make cooking in the air fryer oven easier, safer, and more enjoyable with better results.

Cooking Pan, Air Frying Basket, and Wire Metal Oven Rack

You will cook the majority of the recipes in this book using the black enamel cooking pan or the air frying basket, both of which come with all of the Omni ovens. The oven door is labeled with all of the different smart cooking programs, showing you which oven rack position to use for each cooking program. For instance, if a recipe uses the **AIR FRY** program, you'll put the wire metal oven rack in the rack position labeled "**Air Fry**" and place the black enamel cooking pan underneath it in the bottom oven rack position to catch any drips or crumbs. If a recipe uses the **BAKE** program, you'll position the cooking pan in the oven rack position labeled "**Bake**."

For recipes that use additional cookware, such as a cake pan or Pyrex baking dish, you'll place the cookware directly on top of the black enamel cooking pan. It provides a much more stable surface than the wire metal oven rack, which is better suited to air frying and toasting.

Large Mixing Bowl

To some people, a 5- or 7-quart bowl may seem like an absurdly large thing to have in your kitchen, especially if your household is small like mine. However, I find it immensely helpful to have a big bowl for tossing vegetables in their oil and seasonings before air frying. It's much easier to achieve an even-all-around coating of oil and seasonings when tossing food in a bowl as opposed to drizzling oil on the food while it's already on the pan, then awkwardly flipping or stirring it with your hands or a utensil. Also, your hands stay clean this way.

You can either use a spatula or just hold onto the bowl tightly and use a flick of your wrists to get the food to slide up the side of the bowl, into the air, and back into the bowl again. I learned this method in my catering days, when we'd toss vegetables in oil and herbs for roasting or toss big salads with vinaigrette. And as an added bonus, my toddler thinks it looks super cool.

My favorite large mixing bowls are the lightweight, stainless-steel ones from Vollrath. They make both light- and heavy-duty bowls—the lighter ones are much easier to maneuver, and they're less expensive.

Refillable Oil Spraying Bottle

I keep two spray bottles on my counter, one with extra virgin olive oil and another with cold-pressed avocado oil, since I use those oils most often. There are many brands of spray bottles available in cookware stores and online. Misto brand bottles have been around a long time, and they work well, as do the newer (and more pricey) Evo brand bottles. If you prefer a glass spray bottle, there are many similar-looking and similarly rated ones in different brands available on Amazon, as well.

Of course, you can also use prefilled spray bottles or cans from the grocery store, such as Spectrum, Chosen Foods, PAM, or a store brand. I tend to go through a good amount of oil, though, and I like that I can choose high-quality oils to put in refillable bottles. They're also an eco-friendlier option than cooking spray.

When you are spraying any kind of oil, do not spray it inside the oven—this is a fire hazard. Rather, spray the food before you put it in the oven. Or if the food needs to be sprayed partway through the cooking program, use heat-

resistant mitts to remove the cooking pan or basket from the air fryer oven, spray the food, then return it to the oven.

Heat-Resistant Mitts

Oven mitts are key for safety when you're using an air fryer oven—if you're not wearing them, it is all too easy to burn your hands. Even when I'm just removing toast from the oven, I'll either use tongs or put on heat-resistant mitts. I like the ones with a silicone coating from OXO and Gorilla Grip brands, as they are better insulated than traditional quilted cloth mitts, especially if they become damp. The mini all-silicone oven mitts from Instant Pot and other brands also work well, but they do give you less hand and arm coverage than larger mitts. On the plus side, they're a little more maneuverable. Use whichever kind you prefer.

Stainless-Steel Tongs

I find that it's much easier to get a grip on foods with tongs that have stainless-steel heads rather than ones that are made of nylon or coated in silicone. Any tongs will work, though, so use whichever kind you prefer. They are the perfect tool for tossing, flipping, and grabbing foods. I also use them to grab the edge of the hot air frying basket and scoot it closer to the front of the oven so that it's easier to remove safely. There are many brands of stainless-steel tongs available—just look for ones that have a nonslip grip on the handles for easier operation.

Thin Flexible Spatula

My favorite spatula to use for turning foods in the air fryer oven is the thin flexible nylon turner from OXO. It's heat resistant up to 400°F, and the extremely thin edge is so easy to get under breaded foods like chicken tenders (page 179) without gouging or scraping off any of the breading. It's also sturdy enough to lift heavier items like burgers (page 145) and pork chops (page 161).

Metal Baking Pans

The Omni ovens accommodate a wide variety of cookware that you probably already have in your kitchen. Besides the black enamel cooking pan that comes with the appliance, you can use quarter sheet pans, round cake pans of most sizes, loaf pans, 8- and 9-inch square baking pans, and some metal 9×13-inch baking pans, provided they don't have handles that stick out from the sides. Having an arsenal of different-size pans will set you up to bake, broil, and roast whatever you like. As a bonus, a quarter sheet pan that comes with a cooling rack makes a convenient setup for breading, as well as cooling baked goods.

For one of my favorite desserts of all time, Basque-style cheesecake (page 247), you'll want to have a 3-inch-tall 7-inch round cake pan. I use the one from Fat Daddio, available on Amazon.

Whichever pan you are using, when baking in the Omni ovens, use the black enamel cooking pan underneath it rather than the wire metal oven rack. This will make for a more stable base for the baking pan.

Pyrex and Corningware Baking Dishes

Any glass or ceramic dish that is oven safe is also air fryer oven safe, provided that it fits in your air fryer oven. A wide variety of Pyrex brand dishes will fit in the Omni ovens. In particular, I enjoy using their 8-inch square baking dishes for slow-cooked dishes like chicken (page 185), as well as baked desserts including brownies (page 264) and mochi (page 266).

Pyrex also has a line of smaller glass baking dishes made especially for toaster ovens and air fryer ovens. They're called Pyrex Littles, and they currently come in 18-, 24-, and 28-ounce sizes. I use the 28-ounce size when I'm making olive oil–poached shrimp (page 195).

For single-serving desserts, ramekins are a great size to fit in your air fryer oven. The 7-ounce ramekins from Corningware make adorable baking and serving dishes for individual pumpkin pies (page 256).

Silicone Muffin Cups

A full-size muffin tin won't fit in most air fryer ovens, but you can still bake a full batch of muffins by using silicone muffin cups. Place as many as you need on top of the black enamel cooking pan to make muffins (page 42), cupcakes (page 245), or egg bites (page 56). I like the silicone muffin cups from OXO best—they have a smooth inner surface that is easy to clean.

Aluminum Foil and Parchment Paper

I find myself using either parchment paper or aluminum foil almost every time I use my air fryer oven.

If you're cooking anything in the air frying basket, the easiest cleanup option is to line the black enamel cooking pan with foil and place it in the lowest rack position of the oven, where it will catch any drips. Tuck the foil under the sides of the cooking pan before sliding it into its rack position, to make sure that the foil doesn't break loose and end up flapping around in the oven.

Parchment paper makes it easy to fry or bake just about anything without fear of it sticking to the air frying basket or cooking pan. Be mindful that when using parchment, especially on the high convection setting, any corners that aren't weighted down by food are liable to flap around. This isn't an issue most of the time, since you can space the food out evenly on the parchment. However, for foods that need to spread when cooking, such as cookies (page 255), I prefer to use aluminum foil, tucked under the edges of the pan.

Instant-Read Thermometer

Especially when you are first getting the hang of cooking in an air fryer oven, it's important to be able to gauge the internal temperature of foods. Taking a quick read with an instant-read thermometer ensures that steaks (page 137), fish fillets (page 209), and other foods are cooked exactly how you like them and have been brought up to a safe temperature. Due to the variability in weight and thickness of cuts of meat and especially seafood, it is important to go by the internal temperature of the food rather than the suggested cooking time in a recipe. Another variable is how cold the food is when you place it in the oven. For instance, if the steaks still have some chill from the fridge, they will surely take longer than ones that have been out on the counter for an hour. Use a thermometer and you'll never have to second guess.

My favorite instant-read thermometers are from the ThermoWorks brand. Their Thermapen thermometers run $80 to $100 depending on the model, which is not cheap, but they are extremely durable workhorses in the kitchen. You can also pick up their less-expensive ThermoPop model for under $35. It works great; it just takes a couple seconds longer to get an accurate temperature read than the pricier Thermapen.

There are plenty of even less expensive instant-read thermometers available in cookware stores and online as well.

You'll see me give instructions throughout this book to use a 1½-tablespoon or 3-tablespoon cookie scoop. These volumes correspond with standardized disher sizes #40 and #20, respectively. The ones I use are the medium- and large-size cookie scoops from OXO.

Shallow Bowls for Breading

Many air fryer recipes involve breading—that is, dredging items in flour, egg wash or another liquid, and finally bread crumbs—for a crispy coating. You don't need specialized bowls or dishes made just for breading foods; any three shallow bowls will do as long as they are large enough to fit the food you are breading. It's easiest to create a breading station with your bowls all lined up before you start dipping, so that things don't get too messy along the way.

Large Silicone Trivet/Mat

It's not a complete necessity, but many people like to avoid grease dripping on the inside of the oven door when taking the air frying basket in and out of the oven. So they place a heat-resistant silicone trivet on top of the oven door when it is open. There are a few brands of these heat-resistant, oven- and dishwasher-safe 9×12-inch silicone trivets available online. You can also place one on the countertop for setting down the air frying basket or cooking pan when you take it out of the oven.

Cookie Scoops

I use a cookie scoop in many recipes in this book, including much more than just cookies. Technically called dishers in restaurant-speak, these scoops are invaluable for measuring out consistently even portions when making meatballs (pages 147, 150, and 163), falafel (page 113), muffins (page 42), and more.

AIR FRYER OVEN PANTRY ESSENTIALS

Here are a few pantry items that I always have on hand to make air fryer oven recipes.

Panko and Plain Bread Crumbs

Bread crumbs make the crunchy coating on so many air-fried foods because, unlike most liquid batters, they don't spread or stick to the air frying basket or cooking pan.

Panko bread crumbs have a very fluffy, extra crispy texture, and they take up about twice the volume, by weight, of traditional bread crumbs. They can't be beat for achieving a crunchy coating on shrimp (page 193), fish fillets (page 209), vegetarian chick'n nuggets (page 127), and more. I like the organic variety from Edward & Sons best, but there are tons of brands available and most are good. Give the crumbs a sniff when you open the container, to make sure they have not gone stale. There are also gluten-free varieties available from Kikkoman and Kinnikinnick.

Traditional plain bread crumbs are smaller than panko, so they make a finer but still crunchy coating. I use them in dishes like eggplant parmesan (page 106) and mozzarella sticks (page 94). I usually have some around because they are very easy to make from leftover bread. Look to page 296 in the Pantry chapter for the recipe—you'll never waste leftover bread again. Another advantage to making your own bread crumbs is that you can use gluten-free bread if you need to. Of course there are also store-bought plain bread crumbs available—the brand I most often use is Progresso, but most brands are just fine. For a gluten-free variety, the Ener-G brand is my favorite.

Spray and Bottled Oils

I use two kinds of oil most often in this book— olive oil and avocado oil. Extra virgin olive oil has a stronger flavor that's suited to Mediterranean cuisines, and avocado oil has a neutral flavor profile and is well suited to high-heat cooking. Any time avocado oil is called for, you can use any neutral-flavored oil that you like. Have some on hand in a bottle for drizzling or adding to foods and some in a spray bottle for lightly coating foods when air frying.

All-Purpose Flour and Leavening Agents

Flour is used in the breading process for many foods, usually as the first step, in order to help the rest of the coating cling to the food. If you prefer, you can always substitute a gluten-free blend for wheat-based all-purpose flour. My favorite gluten-free all-purpose flours are the ones from Cup4Cup, King Arthur Flour, and Bob's Red Mill (their 1-to-1 blend).

For leavening agents, I always keep instant yeast (SAF brand is my favorite) in the fridge or freezer and baking soda and baking powder in the pantry. When you're buying baking powder, choose an aluminum-free variety, such as the ones from Rumford or Bob's Red Mill. This will prevent it adding a metallic taste to foods, especially when it's used in a larger quantity for chicken wings (page 84).

Grains and Beans

Old-fashioned or instant oats make their way into muffins (page 42) and cookies (page 255) in my house often—they're a nutritious whole grain, and I always have at least one or the other variety on hand.

Rice isn't the first thing you think of when air frying, but it's used in arancini (page 72) and stuffed peppers (page 108), and I serve it with tofu (page 124), tempeh (page 122), and lots of other main dishes. I always have at least one short- and one long-grain white rice variety on hand.

Dried chickpeas are the only kind that are suited to making falafel (page 113)—if you use canned, already cooked chickpeas, you'll end up with a mushy, nontraditional texture. You can absolutely use canned chickpeas when you're just crisping them up whole, as in salads (page 129).

I always keep canned or dried black beans on hand for stuffed peppers (page 108) and as a side dish to go with tilapia (page 203) and other Mexican-inspired main dishes. If you like, you can substitute pinto beans in any recipe in this book.

Spice Blends and Rubs

Look to the Pantry chapter in this book for a handful of my favorite homemade spice blends and rubs, or use your favorite store-bought varieties. As far as store-bought blends go, I always have a tin of Old Bay seasoning on hand for seafood recipes, as well as some basic Italian seasoning for meatballs (page 147) and marinara sauce (page 282), a Cajun spice blend for sweet potato fries (page 241), and chili powder for Mexican-inspired recipes.

I love to switch up the flavor profile of different foods with spice blends. Make your own shawarma spice blend (page 290) for Middle Eastern–inspired flavor, mix up a poultry seasoning blend (page 289) for any recipe with turkey, such as burgers (page 188) or roasted

thighs (page 186), or seek out fresh and vibrant spice blends from your local spice shop.

For barbecue rub, I either make my own (page 288) or use one from Traeger or Meat Church, both available online. And for seasoned salt, I make my own (page 291) or reach for a shaker of Lawry's.

Condiments and Sauces

To achieve bold and varied flavors in my recipes, I often rely on strongly flavored condiments from all over the globe. Chinese black bean garlic sauce is an instant flavor bomb for green beans (page 219), Korean gochujang adds sweetness and mild spice to meatballs (page 163), and tahini lends richness and an appealing bitter note to tahina (page 286) and baba ghanoush (page 96). English Worcestershire adds a savory note to meatloaf meatballs (page 150) and tartar sauce (page 277). A little dash of a strongly flavored condiment can really take food up a notch.

To make meals extra special, I make a lot of homemade sauces. They're all easy to throw together, though of course you can use store-bought varieties if you like. I especially enjoy making salsas (pages 274 and 275), and I often whip up my own cashew-based version of mayonnaise (page 276). It's much lighter than egg-based mayo and gives a citrusy lift to anything it goes into.

PRO TIPS: FAQS, DOs, and DON'Ts

If you're new to cooking in an air fryer oven, read through these FAQs and tips first. You'll probably find that some of your own questions are answered here.

Q: I just got my air fryer oven! What should I make first?

A: First, follow the manufacturer's instructions, reading the manual to see if a test run is required. After that, the possibilities are endless. If you want to start with something simple, go for a grilled cheese sandwich (page 119), roasted vegetables (page 216), or chicken wings (page 84). If you're vegetarian or feeding a vegetarian, definitely try my tofu-based chick'n nuggets (page 127)—I can never stop eating them when I make a batch. If you're excited to get into crispy breaded foods, try chicken tenders (page 179) or cashew-crusted mahi mahi (page 200). For an impressive, yet incredibly easy to make dessert, make a beautifully browned Basque-style cheesecake (page 247).

Q: My air fryer oven has a plastic-y smell. Will it go away?

A: Yes. Sometimes air fryer ovens will have a short break-in period, when some of the components release fumes when heated. If this is the case with yours, you can repeat the test run process a few times, allowing the oven to heat and cool until there is no longer any plastic smell. I recommend doing this in a very well-ventilated area or outside if you can!

Q: My air fryer oven says it has an 18-liter capacity. Does that mean I can cook 18 liters of food in it?

A: No, not exactly. That measurement refers to the total volume of the inside of the oven. The cooking capacity is more dependent on the size of the air frying basket and cooking pan or of whatever dish you're using inside the oven.

Q: How do I adjust the cooking time and temperature?

A: Different air fryer ovens have slightly different interfaces. Whether yours has a control panel that's operated with a touch screen, physical buttons, a universal dial, or some combination of these, you'll usually go through a similar set of steps, selecting a cooking program (**AIR FRY** or **BAKE**, for instance), then adjusting the time and temperature according to the recipe.

Q: What if I'm just heating up frozen foods in the air frying basket, like frozen taquitos or corn dogs?

A: My rule of thumb is that, for smaller freezer-aisle items like taquitos, fish sticks, and chicken nuggets, 400°F for 10 minutes on the **AIR FRY** program will usually get you a good result. For thicker or larger frozen foods like veggie burgers and corn dogs or for frozen fries, increase the time to 15 minutes. Once the program ends, I'll use an instant-read thermometer to check the internal temperature on a few pieces of food, making sure everything is nice and hot before serving.

Q: There's steam coming out from the bottom of the oven door. Is that normal?

A: Yes, for foods that contain a lot of moisture, it is totally normal for some steam to escape out of the bottom or sides of the oven door. You may also see some condensation form on the door briefly, as the steam is escaping.

Q: How do I use the rotisserie function?

A: The pork loin (page 154) and whole rotisserie chicken (page 166) recipes make great use of this function and give clear instructions. For more information, look at your air fryer oven manual for instructions on assembling and using the air fryer rotisserie spit. Generally, the rotisserie spit will come with two forks that will grab onto the food and a pair of screws to attach the forks to the spit.

Q: Can I use the rotisserie function without the cooking pan underneath?

A: Yes, you can use the rotisserie function without the cooking pan, but you will need to clean off the bottom heating elements and the crumb tray afterward, thoroughly wiping off any grease. Make sure that you do not turn the oven on while the bottom heating elements or crumb tray have grease or food on them, as this will create smoke.

Q: Can I stack multiple pans/baskets/trays in the air fryer oven at one time?

A: This is also a yes, but foods may not cook as evenly since there will be less airflow getting to the items on the bottom of the oven.

Q: How can I tell when the oven has preheated, when it's cooking, when to turn the food, and when the cooking program has ended?

A: Your air fryer oven should give you both visual and auditory cues for all of these events. The Omni ovens have a convenient cooking status indicator at the top of the control panel telling when the oven is preheating, cooking, or keeping warm, and the oven will beep whenever the status changes. You'll also hear a beep and see the message "**turn food**" on the display when it is time to flip or stir the food. (If a recipe does not state that you should turn or stir the food, ignore this message. The oven will stop beeping on its own, and the cooking program will continue uninterrupted.)

Q: Do I really have to flip all of my air-fried foods during cooking?

A: No, you can skip that step if you'd like. However, the food will be less evenly browned and may not crisp on the bottom.

Q: When does the cooking program pause, and when does it continue?

A: Any time the oven door is opened, a cooking program will pause and the time countdown will pause accordingly. Once you close the oven door again, the program will continue and the time will resume counting down. This means that, for instance, if you are taking food out of the oven to flip it part of the way through cooking, you may want to keep the oven door open a crack, so as to make sure that the cooking program does not count down while you are busy turning the food.

Q: How can I keep from getting burned with my air fryer oven?

A: Always use heat-resistant mitts when taking things out of your oven. Use the appropriate utensil rather than your fingers to grab or flip foods. If you are trying to flip something in the air fryer basket, it is safest to remove the basket from the oven, flip the food, then return the basket to the oven, all while wearing heat-resistant mitts and using the appropriate tool, such as tongs or a thin flexible spatula.

Q: How do I clean my air fryer oven?

A: Usually, wiping down the oven with a damp cleaning cloth will suffice. Look to the next section in this book for some more involved cleaning and care tips.

CLEANING and CARE TIPS

The manuals that come with the Omni ovens recommend cleaning the oven and its accessories after each use. Realistically, this doesn't always happen for me.

If you are intent on keeping your air fryer oven in like-new, sparkling clean condition, you'll want to clean it as often as you can. This will help to avoid grease becoming baked onto the inside walls of the oven, which gets harder to clean off of surfaces the longer and the more times it is heated and cooled.

All of the accessories included with the Omni ovens are dishwasher safe. When you're finished cooking, feel free to place the cooking pan, air frying basket, wire oven rack, rotisserie lift, spit, forks, and screws, and the crumb tray in the dishwasher, if you like. (I prefer to wash the rotisserie parts in a tub in the sink, however, as they are small and easy to lose.)

If you are hand-washing the air frying basket, the best tool for the job is a dish brush rather than a sponge, which can break apart when rubbed on the chrome mesh material. While using a sponge won't damage any of the accessories, the air frying basket material can be hard on sponges! If the basket is especially dirty, soak it in a tub in the sink for a few minutes before scrubbing—it's much easier to remove any cooked-on food after soaking. I also like to spray my basket with Dawn Power-wash Dish Spray before soaking—this helps to release any grease and cooked-on food very easily.

As for the oven itself, check your model's manual to see what types of cleaning products are safe to use. Oven cleaner is fine in some models but not recommended for others. Whatever products you use, unplug the air fryer oven before cleaning.

Most air fryer ovens can be cleaned with a damp cloth and mild dish soap. Giving the oven a final wipe down with a 1-to-3 solution of white vinegar and water (1 part vinegar to 3 parts water) will ensure that any soap residue is removed. Once it is clean, let the oven dry completely before using it again.

For especially tough to remove baked-on grease, Instant Brands recommends spraying on a mixture of baking soda and vinegar, letting it sit for a few minutes, then wiping it off.

HOW TO CONVERT OVEN RECIPES

With this cookbook in your hands, you have over 100 recipes that are specifically written for the Omni ovens. If you'd like to branch out and cook recipes meant for a traditional oven, though, there are some rules of thumb to keep in mind.

Temperature and Time Adjustment

Compared to a traditional oven, an air fryer oven will cook foods much faster, especially on cooking programs with both the top and bottom heating elements turned on. If you try to cook a recipe for a traditional oven in the air fryer without adjusting the temperature, you will usually find that it will overcook or burn on the outside before it is heated through. You will also find that the cooking times for traditional oven recipes are too long for the air fryer oven. **As a rule of thumb, when converting oven recipes for the air fryer, reduce the oven temperature by 25°F and the cooking time by 25 percent.**

One case where I find that this cooking time reduction rule does not always apply perfectly well is with batter-based baked goods made in baking pans or dishes, such as brownies and cakes. For these, I find that the temperature may have to be reduced as much as 50°F, while the cooking time may not have to be reduced significantly. As in a traditional oven, the timing can vary based on the size, type, and material of the baking dish used.

Quantity Adjustment

Keep in mind that when converting recipes for your air fryer oven, you are limited by the capacity of its cookware accessories. You've got about the area of a quarter sheet pan to work with (9×13 inches, or half the size of a half sheet pan). The black enamel cooking pan that comes with the Omni ovens will fit a maximum of about 2 pounds of boneless chicken, 3 pounds of bone-in chicken, or 1½ to 2 pounds of cut-up vegetables.

CHAPTER 1

BREAKFAST & BRUNCH

BLUEBERRY and YOGURT SCONES

VEGETARIAN, GLUTEN-FREE (use GF flour blend)

DAIRY-FREE (substitute coconut oil for the butter and plant-based yogurt for the Greek yogurt)

PREP TIME: 10 MINUTES, PLUS 1 HOUR TO CHILL AND 15 MINUTES TO COOL

COOK TIME: 12 MINUTES

YIELD: 8 SCONES

SCONES

1¼ cups all-purpose flour

2 tablespoons granulated sugar

1 teaspoon baking powder

¼ teaspoon baking soda

⅛ teaspoon kosher salt

4 tablespoons cold unsalted butter, cut into ⅓-inch cubes

⅓ cup full-fat or low-fat Greek yogurt

1 large egg

½ cup fresh or thawed frozen blueberries

GLAZE

½ cup powdered sugar

1 tablespoon lemon juice

½ teaspoon grated lemon zest

Greek yogurt gives these lightly sweetened scones a tender and fluffy crumb. They're topped with a tangy lemon glaze that complements the blueberries. I like to make the dough the night before so all that's left to do is slice and bake the scones in the morning. Serve them at breakfast or with hot tea for a mid-morning treat.

Make the scone dough: In a mixing bowl, stir together the flour, granulated sugar, baking powder, baking soda, and salt until evenly combined. Sprinkle in the butter and use a pastry cutter or a fork to incorporate it into the flour until no larger than pea-size chunks of butter remain and the butter has been mostly worked into the flour.

In a small bowl, whisk together the yogurt and egg until no streaks remain. Pour the egg mixture into the dry ingredients. Use a silicone spatula to gently mix the wet and dry ingredients, just until all of the flour has been absorbed and the dough begins to come away from the sides of the bowl; it will still be a bit crumbly. Gently fold in the blueberries, just until they are evenly incorporated and the dough is no longer crumbly.

Turn the dough out onto a piece of plastic wrap. Pat the dough into a ½-inch-thick disk. Top the dough with another piece of plastic wrap, then tuck in the sides. Refrigerate for at least 1 hour or up to 24 hours.

recipe continues

Preheat the oven on **BAKE** at 325°F and set the cooking time for 12 minutes. Line the cooking pan with parchment paper.

Using a chef's knife or bench scraper, cut the dough into 8 wedges. Place the scones on the cooking pan, spacing them ½ inch apart.

Bake the scones in the preheated oven.

While the scones are baking, make the glaze: In a small bowl, whisk together the powdered sugar, lemon juice, and lemon zest.

Place a cooling rack on a quarter sheet pan.

When the cooking program ends, use a thin flexible spatula to transfer the scones to the cooling rack. While the scones are still warm, drizzle each one with a teaspoon of the glaze. Let the scones cool until the glaze sets, about 15 minutes, then serve.

Nutrition Information: Per scone: 183 calories, 7 grams fat, 27 grams carbohydrates, 1 gram fiber, 4 grams protein

VARIATION If you prefer your scones unglazed, sprinkle on a little bit of coarse turbinado sugar (aka Sugar in the Raw) before baking for a sparkling, crunchy topping.

BAKED APPLE OATMEAL

GLUTEN-FREE (use GF oats)

PREP TIME: 5 MINUTES
COOK TIME: 40 MINUTES
YIELD: 6 SERVINGS

2 tablespoons unsalted butter, melted and cooled, plus more for greasing the pan

2 large eggs

1⅔ cups milk

3 cups old-fashioned oats

¼ cup brown sugar

½ teaspoon ground cinnamon

¼ teaspoon kosher salt

2 tablespoons granulated sugar

¼ teaspoon pumpkin pie spice

2 medium Granny Smith or other baking apples (6 ounces each), peeled, cored, and sliced into ½-inch-thick wedges

Heavy cream or half-and-half, for serving (optional)

This oatmeal has a firm, sliceable texture. With a topping of sweetened spiced apples, it's homey and comforting on a fall or winter morning. Serve it on its own or with a splash of cream or half-and-half poured on top.

Preheat the oven on **BAKE** at 325°F and set the cooking time for 40 minutes. Grease an 8-inch square Pyrex baking dish with butter.

In a mixing bowl, whisk together the eggs and milk until no streaks remain. Add the oats, brown sugar, butter, cinnamon, and salt and stir until well mixed. Pour the mixture into the greased baking dish. Place the baking dish on the cooking pan.

In a small bowl, stir together the granulated sugar and pumpkin pie spice. Arrange the apple wedges on top of the oatmeal in an even layer, then sprinkle the spiced sugar over the apples.

Bake the oatmeal in the preheated oven.

When the cooking program ends, wearing heat-resistant mitts, remove the oatmeal from the oven. Cut the oatmeal into slices and transfer to serving plates. Serve with cream for pouring on top, if you like.

Nutrition Information: Per serving: 237 calories, 9 grams fat, 32 grams carbohydrates, 3 grams fiber, 7 grams protein

ZUCCHINI and CARROT MUFFINS

VEGAN/DAIRY-FREE (substitute flax egg for the egg and plant-based milk for the dairy milk)

GLUTEN-FREE (substitute GF flour blend for the all-purpose flour and use GF oats)

PREP TIME: 10 MINUTES, PLUS AT LEAST 5 MINUTES TO COOL

COOK TIME: 20 MINUTES

YIELD: 9 MUFFINS

¾ cup all-purpose flour

1 teaspoon pumpkin pie spice

¼ teaspoon baking soda

¼ teaspoon kosher salt

1 large egg or 1 flax egg (see note)

¼ cup olive oil

½ cup granulated sugar

2 tablespoons milk

⅓ cup instant or old-fashioned oats

¾ cup grated zucchini

¾ cup grated carrot

A morning treat that's packed with vegetables, sweetness, and spice helps me start the day with a smile on my face, and kids love these, too. Have them warm at breakfast, or pack them for a midmorning snack.

Place 8 silicone muffin cups on the cooking pan, then put a paper cupcake liner in each muffin cup.

In a mixing bowl, whisk together the flour, pumpkin pie spice, baking soda, and salt. Add the egg, oil, sugar, and milk, and whisk to combine, just until all of the flour is absorbed. Use a spatula to fold in the oats, zucchini, and carrot.

Preheat the oven on **BAKE** at 325°F and set the cooking time for 20 minutes.

Use a 3-tablespoon cookie scoop to portion out the batter into the lined muffin cups.

Bake the muffins in the preheated oven.

When the cooking program ends, test the muffins for doneness by inserting a toothpick all the way to the bottom of a muffin, then removing it—it should come out clean.

Remove the cooking pan from the oven and let the muffins rest for 5 minutes, then gently remove them from the muffin cups

You can substitute a flax egg for the egg to make this recipe vegan. In a small bowl, whisk together 1 tablespoon flaxseed meal and 3 tablespoons water, then let sit for 5 minutes to thicken before using.

When I make these for my toddler, I use half the sugar. They still turn out well, and they are considerably less sweet! She loves them with a little bit of cashew butter or peanut butter spread on top, too.

and transfer to a cooling rack. Enjoy warm, or let cool to room temperature, about 30 minutes.

Nutrition Information: Per muffin: 156 calories, 7 grams fat, 22 grams carbohydrates, 1 gram fiber, 3 grams protein

VARIATION If you like, you can make these muffins with all zucchini or all carrot. Use 1½ cups of either one.

MACADAMIA-BANANA FRENCH TOAST

VEGETARIAN, GLUTEN-FREE (use GF bread)

PREP TIME: 10 MINUTES
COOK TIME: 6 MINUTES
YIELD: 6 SLICES

Avocado oil or other neutral-flavored oil, for spraying

FRENCH TOAST
3 large eggs
1 cup buttermilk or milk
½ teaspoon ground cinnamon
½ teaspoon vanilla extract
6 slices Texas toast (see note)

TOPPINGS
3 medium bananas, sliced
⅓ cup roasted macadamia nuts, chopped
1 tablespoon powdered sugar
Maple or coconut syrup, for serving

My husband and I spent our babymoon on the island of Maui, and one of our favorite breakfast spots was a locals' favorite as well, the always busy Kihei Caffe. They serve up generous helpings of French toast topped with crunchy macadamia nuts, sliced ripe bananas, and a shower of powdered sugar. This version comes close, minus the extra calories from what I'm sure are copious amounts of butter used on the flattop grill.

Line the cooking pan with parchment and spray the parchment lightly with oil.

In a blender, combine the eggs, buttermilk, cinnamon, and vanilla. Blend at medium-low speed for about 20 seconds, until smooth. Pour into a shallow bowl. (Alternatively, you can use an egg beater or whisk to beat the ingredients in a mixing bowl until no streaks remain.)

Dunk a slice of bread in the egg mixture, let it soak for 10 seconds, flip it over, and let it soak for another 10 seconds. Let the excess egg mixture drip off for a few seconds, then transfer the soaked bread to the lined cooking pan. Repeat with the remaining bread.

Preheat the oven on **BAKE** at 400°F and set the cooking time for 6 minutes.

recipe continues

NOTES

You can use any other bread you like, such as challah, brioche, or a crusty artisan bread, cut into ¾-inch-thick slices. Depending on the size of the bread, you may not be able to fit 6 slices on the pan at one time—use as much bread as will fit on the cooking pan.

You can also substitute fresh berries or stone fruit for the bananas, if you prefer.

Bake the French toast in the preheated oven. When the "**turn food**" message comes on, use a thin flexible spatula to flip the toast, then return the sheet pan to the oven.

When the cooking program ends, transfer the French toast to serving plates. Top each piece with sliced banana, nuts, and powdered sugar and serve with syrup on the side.

Nutrition Information: Per slice of French toast with toppings: 270 calories, 10 grams fat, 37 grams carbohydrates, 3 grams fiber, 9 grams protein

Per plain slice of French toast: 156 calories, 4 grams fat, 20 grams carbohydrates, 1 gram fiber, 7 grams protein

DENVER OMELET BAKE

GLUTEN-FREE

PREP TIME: 5 MINUTES
COOK TIME: 35 MINUTES
YIELD: 4 SERVINGS

6 large eggs

¼ cup buttermilk or milk

¼ teaspoon ground black pepper

Avocado or other neutral-flavored oil, or cooking spray

8 ounces (2 cups) frozen Tater Tots or 1 batch Home Fries (page 61)

1 cup chopped ham or cooked sausage

1 green bell pepper, diced

½ medium yellow onion, diced

1 cup shredded cheddar cheese

Eggs, ham, peppers, onions, cheese, and potatoes all baked into one easy breakfast casserole. Store-bought Tater Tots or home fries (page 61) make the base, so you can put in as much or as little extra effort as you like! The recipe makes four generous servings, for a filling, protein-packed breakfast.

In a mixing bowl, beat the eggs, buttermilk, and pepper until no streaks remain.

Preheat the oven on **BAKE** at 325°F and set the cooking time for 35 minutes. Grease an 8-inch square Pyrex baking dish with oil or cooking spray.

Sprinkle even layers of the Tater Tots, chopped ham, bell pepper, onion, and cheddar into the baking dish. Pour the egg mixture over the other ingredients. Place the baking dish on top of the cooking pan.

Bake the casserole, uncovered, in the preheated oven.

When the cooking program ends, wearing heat-resistant mitts, remove the baking dish from the oven. Let the bake rest for 5 minutes. Slice into squares and serve warm.

Nutrition Information: Per serving: 383 calories, 23 grams fat, 22 grams carbohydrates, 2 grams fiber, 23 grams protein

COCONUT, HEMP, and CHIA GRANOLA

VEGAN, GLUTEN-FREE (use GF oats)

PREP TIME: 5 MINUTES, PLUS
45 MINUTES TO COOL

COOK TIME: 15 MINUTES

YIELD: 2½ CUPS GRANOLA
(10 SERVINGS)

1½ cups old-fashioned oats

¾ cup unsweetened coconut
flakes

¼ cup hemp hearts

2 tablespoons chia seeds

¼ cup agave nectar or maple
syrup

¼ cup coconut oil or ghee

½ teaspoon vanilla extract

¼ teaspoon ground ginger

¼ teaspoon ground cardamom

¼ teaspoon kosher salt

I've been baking up batches of homemade granola since my college days—it's so fun to customize the ingredients as well as the level of sweetness to your liking. This one is packed with nutritious superfood ingredients to start your morning off right. Aromas of vanilla, ginger, and cardamom will fill your kitchen as it bakes. Look to the note for instructions on making a parfait.

Line the cooking pan with parchment paper.

In a large mixing bowl, combine the oats, coconut, hemp hearts, and chia seeds.

In a small saucepan on the stove over medium-low heat, heat the agave nectar and coconut oil until the coconut oil has melted and the mixture has begun to simmer, about 4 minutes. Turn off the heat and stir in the vanilla, ginger, cardamom, and salt.

Preheat the oven on **BAKE** at 325°F and set the cooking time for 15 minutes.

Pour the agave–coconut oil mixture over the oat mixture. Working quickly before the oats absorb the wet ingredients, use a silicone spoon or spatula to stir until the dry ingredients are evenly coated. Transfer the mixture to the lined cooking pan, spreading it out in an even layer.

You can also add dried fruit to the granola, if you like. Wait until the granola is completely cooled before stirring in up to 1 cup of raisins, cranberries, or diced dried apples, mangoes, pineapples, or apricots.

To make a yogurt parfait: Spoon ¼ cup plain yogurt into a jam jar or drinking glass, followed by 1 tablespoon of any jam or fruit spread, ¼ cup berries or chopped fruit, and 2 table-spoons granola. Repeat the layers once more. Serve right away.

Bake the granola in the preheated oven, stirring every 5 minutes to ensure even browning.

When the cooking program ends, wearing heat-resistant mitts, remove the granola from the oven. Let the granola cool to room temperature on the pan, about 45 minutes. Enjoy right away, or transfer the granola to a tightly lidded container and store at room temperature for up to 2 weeks.

Nutrition Information: Per serving (¼ cup granola): 201 calories, 13 grams fat, 18 grams carbohydrates, 4 grams fiber, 4 grams protein

DUTCH BABY with CINNAMON and PEARS

GLUTEN-FREE (substitute GF flour blend for the all-purpose flour)
DAIRY-FREE (use plant-based milk and substitute vegan butter or coconut oil for the butter)

PREP TIME: 5 MINUTES, PLUS 5 MINUTES TO COOL
COOK TIME: 15 MINUTES
YIELD: 4 SERVINGS

¾ cup milk (any dairy or unsweetened plant-based variety)

⅔ cup all-purpose flour

3 large eggs

3 tablespoons granulated sugar

½ teaspoon vanilla extract

¼ teaspoon kosher salt

2 tablespoons unsalted butter, cut into 4 to 6 thin pats

¼ teaspoon ground cinnamon

1 ripe Anjou or Comice pear (or any soft variety), cut into ½-inch pieces

Lemon wedges, for serving

A funny name for a fun breakfast, the Dutch baby puffs dramatically as it bakes, then deflates almost as quickly when you go to serve it. This one has a tasty topping of pears covered in cinnamon sugar. Don't skip the squeeze of lemon at the table—a little bit of citrus really helps to perk up all of the sweet fall flavors.

In a blender, combine the milk, flour, eggs, 1 tablespoon of the sugar, the vanilla, and salt. Blend on medium-low speed for about 20 seconds, until smooth, scraping down the sides halfway through blending.

Place the butter in an 8-inch round cake pan. Place the cake pan on top of the cooking pan, place the pan in the cold oven, then preheat the oven on **BAKE** at 400°F and set the cooking time for 15 minutes. (The butter will melt in the pan while the oven preheats.)

In a small bowl, stir together the remaining 2 tablespoons sugar and the cinnamon.

When the oven has preheated, wearing heat-resistant mitts, remove the cake pan from the oven. Pour in the batter. Sprinkle the pears over the batter in an even layer, then sprinkle the cinnamon sugar over the pears. Return the pan to the oven.

recipe continues

When the cooking program ends, the Dutch baby will be puffed up; it will fall quickly as it cools. Let it cool for 5 minutes, then use a thin flexible spatula to cut it into wedges. Serve warm, with lemon wedges alongside.

Nutrition Information: Per serving: 250 calories, 9.5 grams fat, 33 grams carbohydrates, 2 grams fiber, 8 grams protein

TWO-INGREDIENT ROLLS with HOLES (Greek Yogurt + Self-Rising Flour)

VEGETARIAN

PREP TIME: 10 MINUTES, PLUS
5 MINUTES TO COOL
COOK TIME: 15 MINUTES
YIELD: 4 "BAGELS"

1 cup self-rising flour, plus
    more for the work surface

1 cup nonfat Greek yogurt

1 large egg

1 tablespoon water

1 tablespoon sesame seeds

A bagel by any other name would taste as good, right? These are not bagels, but they are bagel shaped, and with their satisfyingly chewy texture and toasted sesame topping, they are bagel-y enough to hit the spot when a craving hits. They also take a fraction of the time and effort to prepare as a yeasted and boiled bagel, which is a huge win in my book. Made with a simple dough of self-rising flour and nonfat Greek yogurt, each one has just 150 calories and an impressive 10 grams of protein.

Line the cooking pan with parchment paper.

In a small mixing bowl, use a silicone spatula to combine the flour and yogurt until it forms a soft, slightly sticky dough.

Lightly flour a work surface. Transfer the dough to the surface and divide it into 4 equal pieces. Roll a piece of the dough into a snake about 9 inches long by ¾ inch thick. Bring together the ends of the snake and gently pinch them together to make a loop, then transfer it to the cooking pan. Repeat with the remaining pieces of dough to make 4 bagel-shaped rolls.

Preheat the oven on **BAKE** at 350°F and set the cooking time for 15 minutes.

In a small bowl, beat the egg and water until no streaks remain. Brush the egg wash over the rolls, then sprinkle with the sesame seeds.

recipe continues

If you do not have self-rising flour, you can make it by combining 1 cup all-purpose flour with 1¼ teaspoons baking powder and ¼ teaspoon kosher salt.

You can make these bagels with plain yogurt instead of Greek yogurt, if you like. Increase the flour to 1⅔ cups.

Bake the rolls in the preheated oven.

When the cooking program ends, transfer the rolls to a cooling rack for 5 minutes, then enjoy while warm. (Alternatively, let the rolls cool completely, about 30 minutes, then slice, toast, and serve. They're much easier to slice when cooled.)

Nutrition Information: Per roll: 150 calories, 2 grams fat, 25 grams carbohydrates, 0 grams fiber, 10 grams protein

VARIATIONS Switch up the topping, if you like. Try a sprinkle of cheddar cheese and pickled jalapeños, shredded Asiago cheese and black pepper, or a sprinkle of Everything Bagel seasoning instead of the sesame seeds.

CHEDDAR and GREEN ONION EGG BITES

VEGETARIAN, GLUTEN-FREE

PREP TIME: 5 MINUTES, PLUS
5 MINUTES TO COOL

COOK TIME: 13 MINUTES

YIELD: 8 EGG BITES

Avocado or other neutral-
flavored oil, or cooking
spray

4 large eggs

¼ cup cottage cheese

¼ cup cream cheese

4 green onions, chopped

½ cup shredded cheddar
cheese

The secret to fluffy, creamy egg bites? Lots of cheese and a fairly low cooking temperature, which keeps the eggs from getting tough as they cook. I'll have a couple egg bites as a low-carb breakfast, or enjoy them with toast or tucked into a warm tortilla for a heartier meal. They're also a great baby/toddler food—my friend Heather serves these to her daughter June in the mornings, and she gobbles them right up! Look to the variations for different filling ideas beyond cheddar and green onions.

Line the cooking pan with aluminum foil or parchment paper. Place 8 silicone muffin cups on the pan and grease the muffin cups lightly with oil.

Preheat the oven on **BAKE** at 300°F and set the cooking time for 13 minutes.

In a blender, combine the eggs, cottage cheese, and cream cheese. Blend at medium-low speed for about 30 seconds, until smooth. Add the green onions and cheddar cheese and process for 2 (1-second) pulses, just to combine. Working quickly before the egg mixture has a chance to settle, pour ¼ cup of the mixture into each of the muffin cups.

Bake the egg bites in the preheated oven, taking care to slide the cooking pan into the oven slowly, so you don't slosh the egg mixture out of the muffin cups.

When the cooking program ends, wearing heat-resistant mitts, remove the cooking pan from the oven. Let the egg bites cool in their muffin cups for 5 minutes; they will deflate a bit as they cool.

Pop the egg bites out of the muffin cups. Transfer the bites to serving plates and serve, or let them cool to room temperature and refrigerate for up to 3 days in a tightly lidded container.

Nutrition Information: Per bite: 97 calories, 7 grams fat, 2 grams carbohydrates, 1 gram fiber, 6 grams protein

VARIATIONS Try different cheeses in your egg bites! Substitute an equal amount of Brie, Boursin, or Laughing Cow for the cream cheese, and Monterey or pepper Jack, Colby, or mozzarella for the cheddar.

If you like, you can substitute in different mix-ins for the green onions, as well. Sprinkle in ½ cup of whatever you like—bell pepper, ham, or cooked bacon are good options.

BREAKFAST BURRITOS

VEGETARIAN (substitute ½ pound store-bought vegetarian breakfast sausage or 8 slices of vegetarian bacon for the sausage)

GLUTEN-FREE (use GF tortillas, such as Siete brand)

DAIRY-FREE (substitute unsweetened plant-based milk for the dairy milk, vegan butter for the butter, and vegan cheese shreds, such as Daiya brand, for the cheese)

PREP TIME: 10 MINUTES

COOK TIME: 4 MINUTES TO HEAT THE TORTILLAS, 3 MINUTES TO COOK THE EGGS, AND 8 FOR THE BURRITOS

YIELD: 4 BURRITOS

4 burrito-size flour tortillas (about 10 inches in diameter)

4 large eggs

2 tablespoons milk

½ teaspoon kosher salt

Pinch cayenne pepper (optional)

1 tablespoon unsalted butter

8 ounces (2 cups) Tater Tots, cooked according to instructions on page 234, or 2 cups Home Fries (page 61)

½ batch Breakfast Sausage Patties (page 65), cooked and chopped

¾ cup shredded Monterey Jack, cheddar, or Mexican cheese blend

Salsa Ranchera (page 274), for serving

These burritos make for a hearty start to the day—one of them keeps me full straight through the morning until lunchtime. They're loaded with crispy Tater Tots, flavorful homemade sausage (page 65), fluffy scrambled eggs, and a generous measure of melty cheese. A final foil-wrapped bake ensures that they are piping hot on the inside and makes them portable, too. Serve with homemade Salsa Ranchera (page 274) or your hot sauce of choice.

Warm the tortillas on the stove: Heat a large skillet over medium heat. Warm each tortilla for about 30 seconds on each side, until hot and pliable. Set the tortillas on a dish and cover to keep them warm.

In a mixing bowl, whisk together the eggs, milk, salt, and cayenne (if using). Over medium heat, melt the butter in the skillet you used for the tortillas. Add the egg mixture and scramble, stirring constantly, 2 to 3 minutes, or until just cooked through— they should be a bit glossy in appearance and soft.

Assemble the burritos: Place a tortilla on a work surface, and add one-quarter of the eggs in a line down the bottom third of the tortilla. On top of the eggs, add one-quarter of the hash browns. Sprinkle on one-quarter of the sausage, then one-quarter of the cheese. Fold up the bottom and sides of the tortilla, then roll it into a burrito. Wrap the burrito in aluminum foil and place it on the cooking pan. Repeat with the remaining tortillas, eggs, potatoes, sausage, and cheese.

recipe continues

Preheat the oven on **BAKE** at 400°F and set the cooking time for 8 minutes.

Bake the burritos in the preheated oven.

Wearing heat-resistant mitts, remove the burritos from the oven, unwrap them and transfer to serving plates, or keep them wrapped in foil and take them with you on the go. Serve with salsa on the side.

Nutrition Information: Per burrito: 600 calories, 33 grams fat, 48 grams carbohydrates, 2.5 grams fiber, 26 grams protein

POTATO, CAULIFLOWER, and BELL PEPPER HOME FRIES

VEGAN, GLUTEN-FREE

PREP TIME: 5 MINUTES
COOK TIME: 20 MINUTES
YIELD: 4 SERVINGS (ABOUT 3 CUPS)

½ pound cauliflower florets, cut into ¾-inch pieces (about 2 cups)

½ pound (1 medium) russet potato, cut into ½-inch cubes (about 1¾ cups)

1 red bell pepper, seeded and cut into ½-inch pieces

½ medium yellow onion, diced

1 tablespoon olive oil

½ teaspoon seasoned salt (page 291)

NOTES

These home fries can be substituted for Tater Tots in breakfast burritos (page 59) and casseroles (page 47).

For traditional home fries, omit the cauliflower and use 1 pound (2 medium) potatoes.

These home fries are lighter than most skillet versions, yet they are still full of flavor. The vegetables are tossed with oil and seasoned salt, then baked at high heat until the potatoes are crispy and the cauliflower, bell pepper, and onions are deeply browned. Top each serving of home fries with a fried egg and some sliced avocado for an easy, nutritious breakfast.

Preheat the oven on **BAKE** at 400°F and set the cooking time for 20 minutes.

Combine the cauliflower, potato, bell pepper, and onion in a large mixing bowl. Drizzle with the oil and sprinkle with seasoned salt, then toss well to coat the vegetables. Spread out the vegetables on the lined cooking pan.

Bake the vegetables in the preheated oven.

When the cooking program ends, transfer the home fries to plates and serve right away.

Nutrition Information: 121 calories, 4 grams fat, 20 grams carbohydrates, 5 grams fiber, 3 grams protein

PECAN PRALINE CANDIED BACON

GLUTEN-FREE, DAIRY-FREE (use vegan butter)

PREP TIME: 5 MINUTES, PLUS
2 MINUTES TO COOL
COOK TIME: 13 MINUTES
YIELD: 6 SLICES

6 slices center cut or regular bacon, medium or thick-sliced (do not use very thin bacon)

¼ cup raw pecan halves

3 tablespoons brown sugar

1½ teaspoons unsalted butter

Pinch ground cinnamon

Pinch cayenne pepper (optional)

Pinch salt

The dining scene in Portland, Oregon, caters to a brunch-loving crowd, and one of the hottest tickets in town is a Southern comfort food spot called Screen Door. They serve an addictive side dish of praline bacon with a candied coating of brown sugar and pecans. This is my version, which still tastes incredibly decadent even with leaner center cut bacon and 1½ teaspoons of sugar per slice. The bacon starts in a cold oven, which helps to keep it from curling up as it cooks.

Line the cooking pan with foil. Lay the slices of bacon on the pan in a single layer.

Place the pan of bacon in the cold oven. Set the oven on **BAKE** at 375°F and set the cooking time for 8 minutes.

While the oven is preheating, combine the pecans, brown sugar, butter, cinnamon, cayenne (if using), and salt in a mini chopper. Process in 8 (1-second) pulses, until you can still see little pieces of pecans, but the mixture is beginning to clump together.

When the oven has preheated, wearing heat-resistant mitts, remove the pan from the oven. Sprinkle about 2 teaspoons of the pecan topping down the center of each slice of bacon, then press it down so it spreads out almost to the edges of each slice.

Place the bacon back in the oven and let cook for the remaining 8 minutes.

recipe continues

NOTE

This method also works well for plain bacon, without the praline topping. Start it in a cold oven, as written, and cook for 8 minutes, or 10 minutes if you want it extra crispy. For thin bacon, adjust the cooking time to 6 minutes.

When the cooking program ends, use tongs to grasp the end of each piece of bacon and slide it onto a serving platter or plates while still hot and pliable (this will keep the topping from cracking). Let the bacon cool for about 2 minutes, then serve warm.

Nutrition Information: Per slice: 92 calories, 6 grams fat, 7 grams carbohydrates, 0 grams fiber, 3 grams protein

BREAKFAST SAUSAGE PATTIES

GLUTEN-FREE, DAIRY-FREE

PREP TIME: 5 MINUTES
COOK TIME: 8 MINUTES
YIELD: ABOUT 1 POUND SAUSAGE,
8 LARGE PATTIES

1 pound ground pork (80% lean), chicken, or turkey (85% or 93% lean)

1 tablespoon maple syrup or brown sugar

1 teaspoon garlic powder

1 teaspoon dried sage leaves

1 teaspoon fennel seeds

½ teaspoon ground black pepper

½ teaspoon Aleppo pepper flakes (optional; see note)

⅛ teaspoon ground allspice

1 teaspoon kosher salt

NOTES
The sausage mixture can be made up to 24 hours in advance and refrigerated, covered. This helps the flavors blend together, too, so it's actually preferable to cooking them right away, if you can plan ahead.

Aleppo pepper is less spicy than regular red pepper flakes, but it still adds a nice kick of spice. Use a scant ½ teaspoon red pepper flakes, or add ⅛ teaspoon cayenne pepper instead.

When you make your own breakfast sausage, you get to control the seasoning as well as the variety and leanness of the meat—ground pork, chicken, and turkey all work well, with whatever percentage of lean to fat that you prefer. A custom mix of spices adds so much flavor, especially the aromatic whole fennel seeds, which pair perfectly with the sweetness of maple syrup. Serve the sausage patties on a plate alongside scrambled eggs and hash browns, or chop them to use in Breakfast Burritos (page 59).

In a large mixing bowl, combine the meat, maple syrup, garlic powder, sage, fennel seeds, black pepper, Aleppo pepper (if using), allspice, and salt. Use your hands to mix everything together until evenly combined.

Preheat the oven on **BAKE** at 425°F and set the cooking time for 8 minutes. Line the cooking pan with parchment paper.

Using a large (3-tablespoon) cookie scoop, portion out 8 scoops of the sausage mixture onto the lined cooking pan. Use your fingers to pat the sausage down into patties about ⅓ inch thick, making a divot in the center of each one.

Bake the sausage patties in the preheated oven.

When the cooking program ends, use a spatula to transfer the patties to serving plates and serve.

Nutrition Information: Per patty (using 80% lean ground pork): 151 calories, 11 grams fat, 3 grams carbohydrates, 0 grams fiber, 10 grams protein

CHAPTER 2

SNACKS & APPETIZERS

FAST FOCACCIA with SPICY CHEESE SPREAD

VEGETARIAN, VEGAN/DAIRY-FREE
(substitute Cashew Garlic and Herb
Cream Cheese on page 287 for the
cream cheese and vegan cheese
shreds for the cheddar)

PREP TIME: 10 MINUTES, PLUS
15 MINUTES TO COOL

COOK TIME: 40 MINUTES TO PROOF,
15 OR 20 MINUTES TO BAKE

YIELD: 1 (9×13-INCH) FOCACCIA
AND ¾ CUP SPREAD

FOCACCIA

1¾ cups all-purpose flour

¾ cup lukewarm water (110°F)

1½ teaspoons instant yeast

2½ tablespoons olive oil

¾ teaspoon kosher salt

1 teaspoon chopped fresh
   rosemary or thyme leaves,
   Italian seasoning, or za'atar
   seasoning (optional)

SPICY CHEESE SPREAD

½ cup cream cheese

½ cup finely shredded medium
   or sharp cheddar cheese

½ teaspoon Tabasco sauce,
   plus more to taste

Small pinch cayenne pepper

This recipe is inspired by fond memories of the breadsticks and cheese spread served for "hot lunch" at my middle school, catered by Florentine, a now-closed Italian-American restaurant in Los Altos, California. The warm, herbed bread and tangy spread are as irresistible a combination now as they were then. Best of all, this is the fastest focaccia you'll ever make, in about an hour start to finish—the dough proofs in the air fryer oven, then bakes in 15 to 20 minutes, depending on how crispy you like your bread.

Make the focaccia dough: In a mixing bowl that will fit in your oven, combine the flour, water, yeast, 1½ tablespoons of the oil, and ½ teaspoon of the salt. Use a dough whisk or spatula to work the ingredients into a fairly wet, sticky dough, about 3 minutes. Scrape down the sides of the bowl so that the dough is in a ball at the bottom of the bowl.

Cover the bowl tightly with plastic wrap or a silicone lid, and place the bowl in the oven. Select **PROOF** or **DEHYDRATE** at 90°F and set the time for 40 minutes.

When the program ends, the dough should have about doubled in volume.

Line a quarter sheet pan with parchment paper. Drizzle the parchment with 1½ teaspoons of the oil and spread it around. Use

recipe continues

a spatula to transfer the dough to the middle of the parchment—it will be very sticky.

Preheat the oven on **BAKE** at 360°F and set the cooking time for 15 minutes for a softer bread, or 20 minutes for a crunchier, more golden-brown crust.

Drizzle the dough with the remaining 1½ teaspoons oil, then use your fingers to spread and prod the dough out in a ½-inch-thick rectangle. With your fingertips, poke dimples all over the dough. Sprinkle the remaining ¼ teaspoon salt evenly over the dough. If you like, this is the time to sprinkle the dough with the herbs. Place the sheet pan on top of the cooking pan.

Bake the focaccia in the preheated oven.

While the bread is baking, make the spread: Microwave the cream cheese for 30 seconds, until it is a little bit warm. Add it to a mini chopper along with the cheddar, Tabasco, and cayenne. Process for about 2 minutes, until very smooth, scraping down the sides halfway through. Taste for seasoning, adding more Tabasco if you like. Transfer the spread to a ramekin.

When the cooking program ends, wearing heat-resistant mitts, transfer the focaccia to a cooling rack. Let cool for 15 minutes. Slice into rectangles and serve warm, with the cheese spread alongside.

Nutrition Information: Per ⅙ focaccia loaf: 173 calories, 6 grams fat, 27 grams carbohydrates, 2 grams fiber, 6 grams protein

Per 2 tablespoons cheese spread: 102 calories, 10 grams fat, 1 gram carbohydrates, 0 grams fiber, 4 grams protein

GARLIC and HERB KNOTS

VEGAN (omit parmesan)

PREP TIME: 10 MINUTES
COOK TIME: 10 MINUTES
YIELD: 8 KNOTS

1½ tablespoons olive oil or unsalted butter, melted and cooled

1 tablespoon chopped fresh parsley

1 teaspoon chopped fresh rosemary

2 cloves garlic, pressed or grated on a Microplane

¼ teaspoon kosher salt

Flour, for the work surface

½ batch Refrigerator Pizza Dough (page 295) or 1 pound store-bought pizza dough

2 tablespoons grated parmesan cheese (optional)

1 cup marinara sauce (page 282), for serving

A classic pizza parlor appetizer you can make at home faster than delivery. Every time I make these, I can't stop eating them! The fluffy, chewy knots of dough are brushed with a mixture of olive oil, garlic, and fresh herbs and, if you like, showered with parmesan cheese before serving. Bake a batch to go with pizza (page 116), or serve them in place of bread rolls with any dinner.

Line the cooking pan with parchment paper.

In a bowl, stir together the oil, parsley, rosemary, garlic, and salt.

Lightly flour a work surface. Place the pizza dough on the surface, then use a bench scraper or chef's knife to divide the dough into 8 equal pieces.

Roll out a piece of dough into a 6-inch-long rope. Briefly roll it around in the bowl of flavored oil to coat it with the oil and herbs. Tie the dough into a knot, then place it on the lined cooking pan. Repeat with the rest of the dough to make 8 knots.

Preheat the oven on **BAKE** at 375°F and set the cooking time for 10 minutes. Bake the knots in the preheated oven.

When the cooking program ends, wearing heat-resistant mitts, remove the pan of knots from the oven. Transfer the knots to a serving platter or plates, top with parmesan (if using), and serve with marinara sauce on the side.

Nutrition Information: Per knot: 129 calories, 3 grams fat, 22 grams carbohydrates, 0 grams fiber, 4 grams protein

ARANCINI (Cheese-Stuffed Risotto Balls)

VEGETARIAN, GLUTEN-FREE (use GF panko bread crumbs)

PREP TIME: 10 MINUTES, PLUS 15 MINUTES TO COOL THE RISOTTO AND 1 HOUR TO CHILL

COOK TIME: 30 MINUTES FOR THE RISOTTO, AND 12 MINUTES FOR THE ARANCINI

YIELD: 12 ARANCINI

RISOTTO

1 tablespoon unsalted butter

1 tablespoon olive oil

1 shallot, minced

¾ cup Arborio rice

1¾ cups low-sodium chicken broth

¼ cup grated parmesan cheese

⅛ teaspoon ground black pepper

ARANCINI

2 ounces low-moisture mozzarella (string cheese works great), cut into 12 (½-inch) cubes

1 large egg

⅔ cup panko bread crumbs

½ teaspoon Italian seasoning

Olive oil, for spraying

1 batch Roasted Marinara Sauce (page 282) or 2 cups store-bought marinara sauce, warmed, for serving

Use your Instant Pot to make a basic batch of creamy risotto, then roll it up into air-fried arancini. I've been preparing pressure cooker risotto for years, but using it for these crispy air-fried treats adds a whole new level of deliciousness. The little balls of risotto surround a molten mozzarella center, and a coating of panko bread crumbs gives them a golden, crispy exterior. These are on the small side, so you can serve them as a passed appetizer or at the table.

Make the risotto in an Instant Pot: Select the **SAUTE** program on an Instant Pot and heat the butter and oil.

When the butter has melted, add the shallot. Sauté until the shallot is a bit softened, about 2 minutes. Stir in the rice and sauté for another minute. Stir in the broth. Scrape down the sides of the pot to make sure all of the rice is submerged in the broth.

Secure the lid and set the Pressure Release to **Sealing**. Select the **PRESSURE COOK** or **MANUAL** program and set the cooking time to 8 minutes at high pressure. (The pot will take about 10 minutes to come up to pressure before the cooking program begins.)

When the cooking program ends, let the pressure release naturally for 10 minutes. Move the Pressure Release from **Sealing** to **Venting** to release any remaining steam.

When the pressure has fully released, open the pot and stir in the parmesan and pepper. Spread out the risotto in an even layer on

a quarter sheet pan and let cool for about 15 minutes, until it has cooled enough for you to touch but is still warm and pliable.

Make the arancini: Push the cooled risotto to one end of the quarter sheet pan. Use a 3-tablespoon cookie scoop to portion the risotto into 12 balls. Place a ball in your hand, make an impression in the middle, place 1 cube of the mozzarella in the impression, then press the risotto around it, rolling it into a ball and

recipe continues

completely encasing the mozzarella. Place the ball back on the sheet pan and repeat with the rest of the risotto balls and mozzarella. Cover the sheet pan with plastic wrap and place in the fridge for at least 1 hour or up to overnight.

Create a breading station with two shallow bowls: In the first bowl, whisk the egg until no streaks remain. In the second bowl, stir together the bread crumbs and Italian seasoning until evenly mixed.

Line the air frying basket with parchment paper.

Dredge an arancino in the egg, holding it over the bowl for a few seconds to let any excess egg drip back into the bowl. Next, place the arancino in the bread crumbs, tossing it to coat evenly. Transfer the arancino to the lined air frying basket and repeat with the remaining balls. Spray the arancini with a light coating of oil.

Place the black enamel cooking pan in the bottom oven rack position. Place the wire metal oven rack in the second highest position. Preheat the oven on **AIR FRY** at 375°F and set the cooking time for 12 minutes.

Air fry the arancini in the preheated oven.

When the cooking program ends, using a spatula, gently transfer the arancini to a serving platter or plates. Serve right away, with marinara sauce for dipping.

Nutrition Information: Per arancino: 106 calories, 5 grams fat, 12 grams carbohydrates, 0 grams fiber, 4 grams protein

SOURDOUGH GARLIC BREAD

VEGAN (substitute vegan butter for the butter and omit the parmesan)
GLUTEN-FREE (use GF bread)

PREP TIME: 5 MINUTES
COOK TIME: 5 MINUTES
YIELD: 6 SLICES

3 tablespoons unsalted butter, room temperature

3 cloves garlic, pressed or minced

2 tablespoons chopped fresh parsley

½ teaspoon paprika

½ teaspoon Italian seasoning

½ teaspoon kosher salt

¼ teaspoon ground black pepper

6 (¾-inch-thick) slices crusty sourdough or other artisan bread (about 2 ounces each)

3 tablespoons grated parmesan cheese (optional)

Made with crusty artisan sourdough, fresh garlic, and parsley, this garlic bread comes together in about 10 minutes and tastes so much better than any store-bought garlic bread. You can serve it as an appetizer or side dish with steak (page 137), roasted chicken (page 166), or eggplant parmesan (page 106). On nights when I'm not up for cooking, my husband, Brendan, will bake a batch of garlic bread and heat up some frozen Trader Joe's cioppino, and dinner is served.

Preheat the oven on **BAKE** at 375°F and set the cooking time for 5 minutes. Line the cooking pan with parchment paper or aluminum foil.

In a small bowl, combine the butter, garlic, parsley, paprika, Italian seasoning, salt, and pepper. Use a fork to mash and mix until well combined. Spread about 2 teaspoons of the garlic butter mixture onto each slice of bread. Sprinkle 1½ teaspoons of the parmesan onto each slice of bread over the garlic butter mixture, if you like. Place the garlic bread on the lined cooking pan.

Bake the bread in the preheated oven.

When the cooking program ends, transfer the bread to serving plates and serve.

Nutrition Information: Per slice: 181 calories, 7 grams fat, 24 grams carbohydrates, 1 gram fiber, 5 grams protein

VEGETABLE EGG ROLLS

VEGETARIAN

PREP TIME: 25 MINUTES
COOK TIME: 12 MINUTES
YIELD: 12 ROLLS

1½ ounces bean thread noodles (¼ of a 6-ounce package)

2 teaspoons toasted sesame oil

2 cloves garlic, pressed or minced

½ medium head green cabbage, cored, quartered, and sliced thinly (about 4 cups)

1 stalk celery, sliced thinly

1 medium carrot, peeled and grated

2 green onions, sliced thinly

2 tablespoons oyster-flavored sauce (check that ingredients are vegetarian)

1 tablespoon soy sauce

¼ teaspoon ground black pepper

1 tablespoon cornstarch

1 tablespoon water

12 store-bought egg roll wrappers

Avocado oil or other neutral-flavored oil, for spraying

Sweet Chili Garlic Sauce (page 285), for serving

A Chinese-American takeout staple, egg rolls are a crowd-pleasing crispy appetizer. These are filled with a vegetarian mix of bean thread noodles, cabbage, celery, and carrots, and they're seasoned with savory oyster-flavored sauce, garlic, and toasted sesame oil. The recipe makes a dozen, plenty for four to six people to enjoy at the start of a meal. Use Twin Dragon brand egg roll wrappers if you can find them—they're my favorite for air frying since they get beautifully blistered and browned as they cook.

Soak the bean thread noodles in hot water for 5 minutes, until they are soft and pliable. Drain and rinse the noodles in a fine-mesh colander. Chop them so that the longest pieces are about 2 inches long. Return the noodles to the colander to drain thoroughly.

In a large skillet or wok, heat the sesame oil and garlic over medium-high heat. When the garlic begins to bubble, add the cabbage, celery, carrot, and green onion. Sauté or stir-fry for about 3 minutes, until the vegetables are beginning to wilt and soften. Add the oyster sauce, soy sauce, and pepper and stir to combine. Remove from the heat and stir in the bean thread noodles. Let cool for about 10 minutes, stirring occasionally, until the mixture is no longer piping hot.

In a small bowl, stir together the cornstarch and water to make a slurry.

recipe continues

Lay out an egg roll wrapper with a corner facing toward you. Measure out a packed ¼ cup of the filling and spread it out on the bottom third of the wrapper. Tuck in the bottom and sides of the wrapper and begin to roll away from you. When there is a 1½-inch triangle of wrapper remaining to roll, wet it down with some of the slurry. Roll the rest of the way, then place the egg roll seam side up in the air frying basket. Roll up the rest of the egg rolls and place them in the basket. The fit will be fairly snug, but they should all be able to fit in one layer.

Place the black enamel cooking pan in the bottom oven rack position. Place the wire metal oven rack in the second highest position. Preheat the oven on **AIR FRY** at 375°F and set the cooking time for 12 minutes.

Spray the seam side of the egg rolls with avocado oil, flip them, and spray the other side, leaving them seam side down in the basket.

Air fry the egg rolls in the preheated oven. When the "**turn food**" message comes on, use tongs to flip the egg rolls onto their second side, then return them to the oven.

When the cooking program ends, transfer the egg rolls to a cooling rack. Let cool for 10 minutes. Serve with sweet chili sauce for dipping.

Nutrition Information: Per egg roll: 104 calories, 1 gram fat, 21 grams carbohydrates, 1 gram fiber, 3 grams protein

BUFFALO CAULIFLOWER BITES

VEGETARIAN, VEGAN (substitute ¼ cup Lemony Vegan Mayonnaise, page 276, plus ¼ cup water for the buttermilk, and vegan butter for the butter)

GLUTEN-FREE (use GF panko)

PREP TIME: 5 MINUTES
COOK TIME: 15 MINUTES
YIELD: 4 SERVINGS

½ cup flour

½ cup buttermilk

1 tablespoon avocado oil or other neutral-flavored oil

½ teaspoon garlic powder

¼ teaspoon ground black pepper

¼ teaspoon kosher salt

4 cups 1½-inch cauliflower florets (1 pound, from 1 medium head cauliflower)

⅓ cup panko bread crumbs

Avocado oil, for spraying

¼ cup Frank's RedHot sauce

4 tablespoons unsalted butter, melted

I've tried a lot of different methods for cauliflower bites or "wings," as they're sometimes called, and this is my favorite for both ease of preparation and deliciousness. The cauliflower and batter are stirred up in one bowl, with no extra breading step required. The bites come out beautiful, with bits of crispy panko embedded in the batter. Once they're doused in a classic Buffalo sauce mixture of Frank's RedHot and butter, you'll want to munch on more than your fair share.

In a large mixing bowl, whisk together the flour, buttermilk, oil, garlic powder, pepper, and salt. The batter should be very thick. Add the cauliflower and stir and toss it around very well, for a couple minutes, until the cauliflower is coated in all of its crevices with the batter. Sprinkle the bread crumbs over the cauliflower, then stir so they are evenly distributed.

Line the air frying basket with parchment paper. Place the black enamel cooking pan in the bottom oven rack position. Place the wire metal oven rack in the second highest position.

Preheat the oven on **AIR FRY** at 375°F and set the cooking time for 15 minutes.

Spread out the cauliflower in an even layer in the lined basket. Spray the cauliflower with a light coating of avocado oil.

Air fry the cauliflower in the preheated oven.

recipe continues

I don't find that these need any extra sauce, but you can serve them with store-bought blue cheese or ranch dressing to cool down the spice, if you like. Carrot sticks and celery are traditional accompaniments, as well.

You can use other hot sauce in place of Frank's RedHot if you like. Or you can change up the flavors entirely, forgoing the Buffalo sauce and spooning on some Chinese chili crisp, Middle Eastern za'atar mixed with olive oil, or Indian chaat masala.

While the bites are cooking, in a small bowl, stir together the hot sauce and butter.

When the cooking program ends, use a spatula to transfer the cauliflower bites to a serving platter or plates. Drizzle the Buffalo sauce over the bites, and serve.

Nutrition Information: Per serving: 228 calories, 16 grams fat, 17 grams carbohydrates, 1 gram fiber, 3 grams protein

PÃO DE QUEIJO
(Brazilian Cheese Bites)

GLUTEN-FREE

PREP TIME: 10 MINUTES
COOK TIME: 10 MINUTES
YIELD: 18 BITES

2 cups tapioca flour
(see note)

1 teaspoon kosher salt

⅔ cup milk

¼ cup avocado oil or other
neutral-flavored oil

1 large egg

1 cup grated parmesan cheese

In my travels in Brazil, I enjoyed these chewy, cheesy bread bites many times—they're served just about everywhere. You might know them as Brazi Bites, a popular brand that's sold in the freezer aisle in grocery stores. They're easy to make, and the dough comes together quickly, with no proofing, since the eggs provide plenty of lift. The main ingredient is tapioca flour, which is naturally gluten free. This recipe makes enough for two batches of 9 bites each, so you can freeze half for later.

In a mixing bowl, stir together the flour and salt until evenly combined.

In the microwave or in a small saucepan, heat the milk until it is scalding hot and has just begun to steam (this takes about 1 minute in the microwave), then add it to the bowl with the dry ingredients. Use a dough whisk or wooden spoon to combine—the dough will be very dry and crumbly at this point. Add the oil and egg, and whisk or stir until the batter is smooth. Add the cheese, and stir until combined.

Preheat the oven on **BAKE** at 375°F and set the cooking time for 10 minutes. Line the cooking pan with parchment paper.

Use a 1½-tablespoon cookie scoop to portion out 9 scoops of dough (half of the batch of dough) onto the lined cooking pan.

Bake the pão in the preheated oven.

In Brazil, tapioca flour is commonly available in two varieties: sweet and sour. Sweet tapioca flour is known as regular tapioca flour in the United States. It's located in the baking aisle of most grocery stores, and Bob's Red Mill and Arrowhead Mills are widely distributed brands.

Sour tapioca flour (polvilho azedo in Portuguese) can be difficult to find in stores unless you are in an area with a sizable Brazilian expat population. It is fermented, and it lends a slightly tangy flavor and a higher rise to the pão de queijo. You can order sour tapioca flour online (Yoki and Amafil brands are widely available). Sour tapioca flour is a bit denser than sweet tapioca flour, and so it behaves slightly differently in baked goods. If you use it in this recipe, reduce the quantity to 1¾ cups.

When the cooking program ends, transfer the pão to a serving platter or plates, and serve right away. At this point, you can bake the second batch, or scoop them out onto a quarter sheet pan, freeze for 2 hours, then transfer to a ziplock bag and store, frozen, for up to 3 months. Bake the second batch straight from the freezer—the cooking time will remain the same.

Nutrition Information: Per bite: 85 calories, 4 grams fat, 10 grams carbohydrates, 0 grams fiber, 2 grams protein

LEMON PEPPER PARTY WINGS

GLUTEN-FREE, DAIRY-FREE

PREP TIME: 5 MINUTES
COOK TIME: 25 MINUTES
YIELD: 12 WINGS

1 pound wingettes/party wings/drums and flats (about 12 pieces)

2 teaspoons aluminum-free baking powder (Rumford or Bob's Red Mill brand)

Zest of 1 lemon, grated on a fine Microplane

½ teaspoon ground black pepper

¼ teaspoon kosher salt

¼ teaspoon garlic powder

NOTE
If you would prefer to use store-bought lemon pepper seasoning, note the salt difference between brands and adjust accordingly. For my taste, I like to use 1 tablespoon of Lawry's lemon pepper or 1½ teaspoons of the McCormick version.

Wings are one of the most popular foods to air fry, and for good reason—they come out with well-rendered, crispy skin and tender meat every time. Making your own lemon pepper mixture elevates this appetizer to something really special, and it's as easy as zesting a lemon. Use a fine Microplane so you end up with delicate, fluffy shreds of lemon on every bite.

Pat the wings dry with paper towels. In a large mixing bowl, sprinkle the wings with baking powder. Toss to coat evenly.

Preheat the oven to **AIR FRY** at 400°F and set the cooking time for 18 minutes. Place the black enamel cooking pan in the bottom oven rack position. Place the wire metal oven rack in the second highest position.

Spread out the wings in a single layer in the air frying basket.

Air fry the wings in the preheated oven. When the **"turn food"** message comes on, use tongs to flip the wings, then return them to the oven.

While the wings cook, in a small bowl, stir together the lemon zest, pepper, salt, and garlic powder.

When the cooking program ends, transfer the wings to a clean large mixing bowl and sprinkle on the lemon pepper seasoning. Toss the wings until evenly coated. Transfer wings to a plate and serve right away.

Nutrition Information: Per serving (about 3 wings): 211 calories, 14 grams fat, 0 grams carbohydrates, 0 grams fiber, 20 grams protein

SCOTCH EGGS with MUSTARD SAUCE

GLUTEN-FREE (use GF flour blend and GF panko bread crumbs)
DAIRY-FREE

PREP TIME: 10 MINUTES
COOK TIME: 14 MINUTES
YIELD: 4 EGGS

¼ cup all-purpose flour

1 large egg

1 tablespoon water

⅔ cup panko bread crumbs

2 tablespoons chopped fresh parsley

½ batch uncooked Breakfast Sausage Patties (page 65)

4 large eggs, soft-boiled and peeled (see note)

MUSTARD SAUCE

¼ cup mayonnaise (page 276)

1½ tablespoons stone-ground mustard

1 tablespoon fresh lemon juice

I've had Scotch eggs on a couple of continents, and my favorite version is the one at Radar, a restaurant in Portland, Oregon. They serve this classic appetizer on their brunch menu, and after one bite I knew it would be the perfect candidate for air frying. Soft-boiled eggs are encased in a not-too-thick layer of breakfast sausage, coated with panko bread crumbs, then cooked until they're crispy on the outside, with jammy yolks on the inside. Serve them on their own or with a quick mustard dipping sauce.

Create a breading station with three shallow bowls: Add the flour to the first bowl. In the second bowl, whisk the egg and water until no streaks remain. In the third bowl, stir together the panko and parsley until evenly mixed.

Divide the sausage into 4 equal pieces. Use your hands to flatten a piece of sausage into a ¼-inch-thick patty. Place a soft-boiled egg on top of the patty, then gently mold the sausage around the egg, until it is fully encased. Repeat with the remaining sausage and eggs.

Place the black enamel cooking pan in the bottom oven rack position. Place the wire metal oven rack in the second highest position.

Preheat the oven on **AIR FRY** at 375°F and set the cooking time for 14 minutes.

You can soft-boil eggs in your air fryer oven, in an Instant Pot, or in a pot on the stove. In the air fryer oven, arrange the eggs (in their shells) in the air frying basket, then cook them on **AIR FRY** at 250°F for 15 minutes. In an Instant Pot, pour 1 cup water into the pot, place the wire metal rack in the pot, place the eggs on the rack, then cook using the **PRESSURE COOK** or **MANUAL** program for 3 minutes at high pressure, with a quick pressure release. To soft-boil eggs on the stovetop, cook the eggs in simmering water for 6 minutes. When the eggs are done cooking, transfer them to an ice bath immediately and let cool for 10 minutes, then peel.

Roll a sausage-covered egg in the flour, then the egg wash, then the bread crumbs. Place it in the air frying basket. Repeat with the remaining eggs.

Air fry the eggs in the preheated oven. When the "**turn food**" message comes on, use tongs to flip the eggs, then return them to the oven.

While the Scotch eggs are cooking, make the mustard sauce: In a small bowl, stir together the mayonnaise, mustard, and lemon juice.

When the cooking program ends, transfer the Scotch eggs to serving plates. Serve right away, with mustard sauce on the side.

Nutrition Information: Per serving (1 Scotch egg and 1½ tablespoons sauce): 296 calories, 15 grams fat, 15 grams carbohydrates, 0 grams fiber, 22 grams protein

JALAPEÑO RAREBIT POPPERS

VEGETARIAN, VEGAN/DAIRY-FREE
(substitute vegan cheese shreds for the cheddar and Cashew Garlic and Herb Cream Cheese, page 287, for the cream cheese)
GLUTEN-FREE

PREP TIME: 10 MINUTES
COOK TIME: 6 MINUTES
YIELD: 12 POPPERS

6 large jalapeño chiles
½ packed cup grated sharp cheddar cheese
½ cup cream cheese, room temperature
1 teaspoon whole-grain mustard
¼ cup panko bread crumbs
Olive oil, for spraying
Black pepper, for grinding
1 tablespoon chopped fresh flat-leaf parsley, for serving

Nutrition Information: Per popper: 69 calories, 6 grams fat, 2 grams carbohydrates, 0 grams fiber, 2 grams protein

Traditionally, Welsh rarebit is a savory dish of broiled cheese on toast, but the flavors work perfectly in jalapeño popper form! Sharp cheddar cheese and tangy mustard are mixed in with cream cheese for a rich and tangy filling. Jalapeños add a kick of spice and a lot less calories than a slice of bread, and a sprinkle of panko bread crumbs lends a satisfying, toasty crunch.

Line the cooking pan with foil.

Halve the chiles lengthwise, then use a teaspoon to scoop out their seeds and veins, leaving the top stem intact. Lay the jalapeño halves flat, cut side up.

In a small bowl, stir together the cheddar cheese, cream cheese, and mustard.

Use a mini offset spatula or butter knife to stuff a heaping tablespoon of the cheese mixture into each jalapeño half. Place the stuffed jalapeños cheese side up on the cooking pan.

Preheat the oven on **BAKE** at 400°F and set the cooking time for 6 minutes. Sprinkle each filled jalapeño half with 1 teaspoon bread crumbs, then press them down firmly so they stick to the cream cheese. Spray the poppers lightly with oil, then top each popper with a little grind of black pepper.

Bake the poppers in the preheated oven.

When the cooking program ends, wearing heat-resistant mitts, remove the air frying basket from the oven. Let the poppers rest for 5 minutes, then transfer to a serving platter or plates. Top each popper with a sprinkle of parsley. Serve warm.

BACON-WRAPPED PINEAPPLE BITES

GLUTEN-FREE, DAIRY-FREE

PREP TIME: 10 MINUTES

COOK TIME: 9 MINUTES

YIELD: 12 BITES

4 slices bacon, cut in thirds crosswise

8-ounce piece fresh pineapple (¼ of a large pineapple), cut into 12 chunks

1 tablespoon brown sugar

Pinch cayenne pepper

Sweet and savory, juicy hunks of pineapple are wrapped in bacon with a touch of caramelized brown sugar on top. They're an irresistible one-bite appetizer to serve anytime, but especially spring and summer, when pineapples are at their sweetest. A great addition to any cozy get-together or cocktail party, these are best served warm.

Wrap each piece of bacon around a chunk of pineapple. Place the wrapped pineapple seam side down in the air frying basket. Dollop ¼ teaspoon of the sugar on top of each one and pat it out so it covers the top. Sprinkle the bites evenly with the cayenne.

Place the black enamel cooking pan in the bottom oven rack position. Place the wire metal oven rack in the second highest position.

Preheat the oven on **AIR FRY** at 375°F and set the cooking time for 9 minutes.

Air fry the bites in the preheated oven.

When the cooking program ends, use tongs to transfer the bites to a serving platter, sugar side up. Insert a toothpick in each bite and serve right away.

Nutrition Information: Per bite: 36 calories, 1 gram fat, 4 grams carbohydrates, 0 grams fiber, 2 grams protein

VEGAN STUFFED MUSHROOMS

VEGAN, GLUTEN-FREE (use GF panko bread crumbs)

PREP TIME: 10 MINUTES
COOK TIME: 11 MINUTES
YIELD: 4 SERVINGS

12 large button or cremini mushrooms, stems removed and chopped

1 shallot, minced

2 cloves garlic, pressed or grated on a fine Microplane

2 tablespoons chopped fresh parsley, plus more for serving

½ teaspoon Italian seasoning

¼ teaspoon kosher salt

1 tablespoon olive oil

¼ cup sourdough bread crumbs (page 296) or panko bread crumbs

¼ cup walnuts or pecans, finely chopped

½ cup Cashew Garlic and Herb Cream Cheese (page 287) or store-bought vegan cream cheese, room temperature

Olive oil, for spraying

The vegan filling in these stuffed mushrooms is rich and creamy thanks to cashew cream cheese (page 287), with lots of savory flavor from chopped nuts, garlic, and Italian herbs. Back in my college days, I would bring appetizers like this to our Wednesday vegan potlucks, and nowadays I serve them when I have friends over for dinner. Vegetarians and omnivores alike love them, too.

Preheat the oven on **BAKE** at 400°F and set the cooking time for 3 minutes. Line the cooking pan with parchment paper.

Spread out the chopped mushroom stems on the lined cooking pan. Sprinkle on the shallot, garlic, 2 tablespoons parsley, Italian seasoning, salt, and oil and toss to combine.

Bake the seasoned mushroom stems in the preheated oven.

When the cooking program ends, wearing heat-resistant mitts, remove the pan from the oven. Use a spatula to transfer the cooked mixture to a mixing bowl. Add the bread crumbs, walnuts, and cream cheese and stir to combine. Stuff the mixture into the mushroom caps, then place them back on the lined cooking pan.

Preheat the oven on **BAKE** at 400°F and set the cooking time for 8 minutes.

Spray the stuffed mushrooms lightly with oil, being sure to spray the sides of the caps.

recipe continues

NOTE

When you're shopping for
mushrooms, buy the largest,
firmest ones you can find.
Whether they're button or
cremini, the bigger caps will
make for more impressive bites.
If you are not able to find large
mushrooms (about 2 inches in
diameter), you can still make
this recipe and fill twice as
many medium-size mushrooms.

Bake the stuffed mushrooms in the preheated oven.

When the cooking program ends, transfer the mushrooms to a serving platter or plates. Sprinkle with chopped parsley and serve right away.

Nutrition Information: Per mushroom: 80 calories, 5 grams fat, 6 grams carbohydrates, 1 gram fiber, 3 grams protein

MOZZARELLA STICKS

GLUTEN-FREE (use GF flour blend and GF bread crumbs)

PREP TIME: 10 MINUTES, PLUS
30 MINUTES TO CHILL

COOK TIME: 4 MINUTES

YIELD: 12 MOZZARELLA STICKS

¼ cup all-purpose flour

1 large egg

1 tablespoon water

½ cup plain bread crumbs
     (page 296)

1 teaspoon Italian seasoning

½ teaspoon garlic powder

6 sticks string cheese, cut in
     half crosswise

Olive oil, for spraying

½ cup marinara sauce
     (page 282), warmed, for
     serving

A classic happy hour bar snack, mozzarella sticks are easy to make—and much less greasy when they're air fried. Four minutes might seem like an incredibly short cooking time, but that's really all it takes to get them crispy on the outside and molten on the inside. Serve them right away, while they're still melty and hot.

Create a breading station with three shallow bowls: Add the flour to the first bowl. In the second bowl, whisk the egg and water until no streaks remain. In the third bowl, stir together the bread crumbs, Italian seasoning, and garlic powder until evenly mixed.

Line the air frying basket with parchment paper.

Dredge a cheese stick in the flour, then shake any excess flour back into the bowl. Next, dip the stick into the egg, holding it over the bowl for a few seconds to let any excess egg drip back into the bowl. Place the stick in the bread crumbs, gently tossing to coat it evenly. Finally, do a double-breading step, dredging the crumb-covered stick in the egg wash and the bread crumbs once more. Place the mozzarella stick in the lined basket. Repeat with the remaining sticks.

Place the basket of mozzarella sticks in the freezer for 30 minutes. (This will allow them to firm up a bit and keep from having as many "blow outs" when they air fry.)

Place the black enamel cooking pan in the bottom oven rack position. Place the wire metal oven rack in the second highest position.

Preheat the oven on **AIR FRY** at 375°F and set the cooking time for 4 minutes.

Remove the mozzarella sticks from the freezer. Spray them lightly with oil.

Air fry the mozzarella sticks in the preheated oven. When the **"turn food"** message comes on, use tongs to flip the sticks, spray their second side with oil, then return them to the oven.

When the cooking program ends, transfer the mozzarella sticks to a serving platter or plates. Serve right away, with marinara sauce on the side.

Nutrition Information: Per stick: 72 calories, 4 grams fat, 5 grams carbohydrates, 0 grams fiber, 5 grams protein

ROASTED EGGPLANT DIP
(Baba Ghanoush)

VEGAN, GLUTEN-FREE

PREP TIME: 5 MINUTES
COOK TIME: 20 MINUTES
YIELD: 2 CUPS

1 medium globe or Italian
  eggplant (about 1 pound)
3 tablespoons fresh lemon
  juice
2 cloves garlic, pressed
¼ cup tahini (sesame paste)
½ teaspoon kosher salt
1 tablespoon olive oil
¼ teaspoon smoked paprika
1 batch Yeasted Yogurt
  Flatbreads (page 292), for
  serving

I often think of baba ghanoush as hummus's less popular cousin. It's delicious, though, especially at the height of eggplant season. Baking the eggplant at high heat in the air fryer oven concentrates its sweetness, contrasting with the slightly bitter tahini, tangy lemon juice, and sharp garlic. You can mash the dip with a fork for a rough, rustic texture or blitz it in the food processor if you prefer it smoother. Either way, serve it with warmed flatbreads (page 292) or pitas for scooping.

Preheat the oven on **BAKE** at 425°F and set the cooking time for 20 minutes. Line the cooking pan with parchment paper.

Cut the eggplant in half lengthwise, then place the halves flesh side down on the lined cooking pan.

Bake the eggplant in the preheated oven.

While the eggplant is cooking, in a small bowl, combine the lemon juice and garlic.

When the cooking program ends, wearing heat-resistant mitts, remove the eggplant from the oven. Let the eggplant cool for 15 minutes.

Use your fingers to remove the skin and the tough stem ends of the eggplant halves, then place the peeled flesh in a large bowl (if you want a rough texture) or a food processor (for a smoother texture). Add the lemon juice and garlic, tahini, and salt.

Mash everything together in the bowl with a fork, or process in the food processor for about 30 seconds. Taste for seasoning, adding more salt if needed.

Transfer the baba ghanoush to a serving bowl. Drizzle the oil on top, then sprinkle on the smoked paprika. Serve room temperature or chilled, with flatbread for dipping.

Nutrition Information: Per ¼ cup: 86 calories, 6 grams fat, 6 grams carbohydrates, 2 grams fiber, 3 grams protein

PIE-SPICED APPLE CHIPS

VEGAN, GLUTEN-FREE

PREP TIME: 10 MINUTES, PLUS
10 MINUTES TO SOAK

COOK TIME: 8 HOURS

YIELD: 2 SERVINGS

2 cups water

2 tablespoons lemon juice, or
½ teaspoon citric acid if you
have it on hand

2 medium apples (Jazz, Gala,
and Fuji varieties work well)

½ teaspoon pumpkin pie spice
or ground cinnamon

NOTE
To make a quick version of
these apple chips, cook them on
the AIR FRY setting at 350°F for
10 minutes. They will be softer
and still contain some moisture
and should be eaten right away.

Pack a bag of apple chips as a nutritious alternative to potato chips or other processed snacks for school, work, or a nature hike. These are sprinkled with sweet spices, so they'll fill your house with the smell of pumpkin pie as they're dehydrating. They do take a full 8 hours to dehydrate, so I'll often start them in the evening, then wake up to apple chips the next day.

In a large mixing bowl, combine the water and lemon juice.

Slice the apples very thin, about ⅛ inch thick. (I use a mandoline for this, but you can use a chef's knife; it will just take longer.) Place the sliced apples in the acidulated water and leave to soak for 10 minutes.

Drain the apples, spread them out on a kitchen towel, and pat them dry.

Add the apples to the air fryer basket in as even a layer as possible; it is fine for the slices to overlap. Sprinkle the pumpkin pie spice evenly over the apples. Place the basket on the wire metal oven rack in the oven, then select the **DEHYDRATE** program for 8 hours at 145°F.

When the cooking program ends, remove the basket from the oven and let the apple chips cool to room temperature, about 20 minutes. Enjoy them right away, or store in a tightly lidded container or ziplock bag for up to 2 weeks.

Nutrition Information: Per serving: 80 calories, 0 grams fat, 22 grams carbohydrates, 5 grams fiber, 0 grams protein

SWEET and SPICY BEEF JERKY

GLUTEN-FREE, DAIRY-FREE

PREP TIME: 15 MINUTES, PLUS
20 MINUTES TO CHILL, 12 HOURS
TO MARINATE
COOK TIME: 3 HOURS
YIELD: 8 SERVINGS

1 pound lean steak (such as flank or sirloin), trimmed of any fat

¼ cup soy sauce

2 tablespoons honey

1 teaspoon garlic powder

1 teaspoon red pepper flakes

½ teaspoon ground black pepper

1 teaspoon kosher salt

When you make your own beef jerky, you control the flavors, choosing exactly what you like. In our house, we prefer our jerky lightly sweetened with honey, with a kick of spicy heat from red pepper flakes. You can also decide how chewy you want your jerky to be—cut across the grain of the meat for more tender pieces or with the grain for extra chewy strips.

Place the steak in the freezer to chill for 20 minutes. (This will make it firmer and easier to slice.)

While the steak is in the freezer, make the marinade: In a large shallow dish or a 1-quart ziplock bag, stir together the soy sauce, honey, garlic powder, red pepper flakes, black pepper, and salt.

Using a sharp chef's knife, slice the steak into strips. Cut against the grain for more tender jerky, or with the grain for more chewy jerky, into strips that are ⅛ to ¼ inch thick and about 6 inches long. Add the steaks to the marinade, cover the dish or close the bag, and toss evenly to coat. Marinate in the refrigerator for at least 12 hours or up to overnight.

Lay the marinated beef strips on a paper towel and pat them dry, then arrange them in the air frying basket in a single layer. Discard the marinade.

NOTE

For spicier jerky, replace 1 tablespoon of the honey with gochujang or sriracha sauce. For milder jerky, use gochugaru (Korean red pepper flakes) in place of regular red pepper flakes.

Place the air frying basket on the wire metal oven rack in the oven, then select **DEHYDRATE** at 160°F for 3 hours. After 1½ hours, flip the jerky for more even drying.

When the cooking program ends, remove the air frying basket from the oven. Enjoy right away, or allow the jerky to cool completely, about 45 minutes, then store in a tightly lidded container for up to 1 week.

Nutrition Information: Per serving (1 ounce): 106 calories, 3 grams fat, 5 grams carbohydrates, 0 grams fiber, 13 grams protein

CHAPTER 3

VEGETARIAN

PUFF PASTRY ZUCCHINI TART

PREP TIME: 10 MINUTES
COOK TIME: 12 MINUTES
YIELD: 6 SERVINGS

1 sheet store-bought puff pastry (see note), thawed

1 cup Cashew Garlic and Herb Cream Cheese (page 287; see note), room temperature

¾ pound (2 medium) zucchini, sliced thinly on the bias

Olive oil, for spraying

¼ teaspoon kosher salt

⅛ teaspoon ground black pepper

2 teaspoons chopped parsley, for garnish

NOTES
Puff pastry is traditionally made with butter, so read the label if you want to make sure the tart is vegan. Pepperidge Farm brand does not use butter.

You can substitute store-bought plain vegan or dairy cream cheese for the cashew cream cheese, if you like. Stir in ½ teaspoon Italian seasoning and ¼ teaspoon garlic powder.

Serve slices of this flaky and flavorful tart for lunch or as an appetizer or first course. It looks beautiful and impressive but is so, so easy to make. The garlic and herb cream cheese is made from cashews, and it acts as a creamy base for tender slices of zucchini, all on top of flaky, rich, and surprisingly vegan puff pastry.

Line the cooking pan with parchment paper. Unfold the puff pastry and place it on the lined pan. Use a mini offset spatula or butter knife to spread out the cream cheese over the pastry in an even layer, leaving a ½-inch border on all sides. Arrange the zucchini on top of the cream cheese in an overlapping pattern.

Preheat the oven on **BAKE** at 400°F and set the cooking time for 12 minutes.

Spray the zucchini lightly with oil, then sprinkle with the salt and pepper.

Bake the tart in the preheated oven.

When the cooking program ends, slide the tart onto a cutting board and sprinkle it with the parsley. Cut the tart into 6 slices, transfer to serving plates, and serve right away.

Nutrition Information: Per serving: 300 calories, 24 grams fat, 18 grams carbohydrates, 2 grams fiber, 4 grams protein

EGGPLANT PARMESAN

GLUTEN-FREE (use GF flour and bread crumbs)

PREP TIME: 20 MINUTES, PLUS 45 MINUTES TO SALT THE EGGPLANT

COOK TIME: 13 MINUTES FOR THE SLICES, 12 MINUTES FOR THE CASSEROLE

YIELD: 4 SERVINGS

1 large globe or Italian eggplant (1¼ pounds)

1 teaspoon kosher salt

Olive oil, for spraying

⅓ cup all-purpose flour

2 large eggs

2 tablespoons water

⅓ cup plain bread crumbs

⅓ cup grated parmesan cheese

1½ teaspoons Italian seasoning

1 teaspoon garlic powder

1½ cups marinara sauce (page 282)

1 cup shredded mozzarella cheese

Eggplant parmesan is very easy to make, especially in the air fryer! Crispy breaded cutlets are baked in a casserole with marinara sauce and plenty of mozzarella cheese. The eggplant is salted before breading, which helps draw some of the liquid out and makes the texture extra silky, just like versions that use a lot more oil. This step takes a little extra time but saves so many calories and makes a huge improvement in the finished dish. Serve it as a vegetarian main dish, with crusty bread or a green salad alongside.

Cut the eggplant into about 12 (½-inch-thick) rounds and place them on a cooling rack on top of a quarter sheet pan. Sprinkle the eggplant slices evenly with the salt on both sides. Leave the salted eggplant to sit for 45 minutes—it will weep a bit of moisture as it sits.

Rinse the slices of eggplant under running water, then pat them dry with a kitchen towel.

Line the cooking pan with parchment paper and spray the parchment lightly with oil.

Create a breading station with three shallow bowls: Add the flour to the first bowl. In the second bowl, whisk the eggs and water until no streaks remain. In the third bowl, stir together the bread crumbs, parmesan, Italian seasoning, and garlic powder until evenly mixed.

Dredge 1 slice of eggplant in the flour, then shake any excess flour back into the bowl. Next, dip the eggplant in the egg mixture, holding it over the bowl for a few seconds to let any excess egg drip back into the bowl. Finally, place the eggplant in the bowl of bread crumbs and gently flip it over a couple times, making sure to coat both sides evenly. Transfer the breaded eggplant to the lined pan. Repeat with the remaining slices.

Preheat the oven on **BAKE** at 350°F and set the cooking time for 13 minutes.

Spray the eggplant slices lightly with oil.

Bake the eggplant slices in the preheated oven.

When the cooking program ends, wearing heat-resistant mitts, remove the cooking pan from the oven.

Ladle ½ cup of the marinara sauce into an 8-inch square Pyrex baking dish. Place half of the eggplant slices on top of the sauce, then ladle on another ½ cup of sauce on top of the eggplant, and sprinkle ½ cup of the cheese evenly over them. Repeat a layer of eggplant, sauce, and cheese. Discard the used parchment paper, then place the baking dish on top of the cooking pan.

Preheat the oven on **BAKE** at 350°F and set the cooking time for 12 minutes.

Bake the casserole in the preheated oven.

When the cooking program ends once again, wearing heat-resistant mitts, remove the baking dish from the oven. Cut the eggplant parmesan into quarters and serve.

Nutrition Information: Per serving: 336 calories, 16 grams fat, 32 grams carbohydrates, 6 grams fiber, 18 grams protein

STUFFED PEPPERS with RICE and BLACK BEANS

VEGETARIAN, VEGAN (substitute vegan cheese shreds for the mozzarella)
GLUTEN-FREE

PREP TIME: 10 MINUTES
COOK TIME: 20 MINUTES
YIELD: 6 SERVINGS

3 extra large red bell peppers (10 ounces each)

2 tablespoons olive oil

2 cloves garlic, pressed

1 small yellow onion, diced

1 jalapeño or serrano chile, seeded and diced

½ teaspoon ground cumin

½ teaspoon ground coriander

½ teaspoon dried oregano

½ teaspoon kosher salt

3 cups cooked rice or quinoa

1½ cups cooked black beans or pinto beans (from a 15-ounce can, rinsed and drained)

Grated zest and juice of 1 lime (3 tablespoons juice)

4 tablespoons chopped fresh cilantro

1 cup shredded mozzarella cheese or Mexican cheese blend

I make stuffed peppers anytime we have leftover cooked rice in the fridge, which is often. Lime, cilantro, coriander, and cumin are added to the rice and beans for a Mexican-inspired flavor that's different from the usual chili powder and tomatoes. Of course, you can also cook the grains to make this recipe specifically (1 cup raw yields 3 cups cooked, prepared according to the package instructions), and you can use quinoa, farro, barley, or whatever grains you have on hand in place of rice, if you like.

Line the cooking pan with aluminum foil or parchment paper.

Halve the bell peppers lengthwise, keeping their stem ends intact. Use a paring knife to carve out and remove the seeds and veins. Place the pepper halves skin side down on the cooking pan.

Make the filling on the stovetop: Add the oil and garlic to a skillet and place it over medium heat. When the garlic begins to bubble, add the onion and jalapeño and sauté until the onion begins to soften, about 2 minutes. Add the cumin, coriander, oregano, and salt and sauté for 1 more minute, until the spices are aromatic. Turn off the heat, then stir in the rice, beans, lime zest and juice, and 3 tablespoons of the cilantro.

recipe continues

Preheat the oven on **BAKE** at 340°F and set the cooking time for 20 minutes.

Stuff ¾ cup of the filling into each pepper half.

Bake the peppers in the preheated oven. When the **"turn food"** message comes on, sprinkle the cheese over the peppers, then return them to the oven.

When the cooking program ends, sprinkle the peppers with the remaining tablespoon cilantro. Transfer them to serving plates and serve.

Nutrition Information: Per serving: 297 calories, 9 grams fat, 46 grams carbohydrates, 6 grams fiber, 12 grams protein

GREEN CHILE and CHEESE BAKE

GLUTEN-FREE (use GF flour blend)

PREP TIME: 5 MINUTES
COOK TIME: 1 HOUR 10 MINUTES
YIELD: 6 SERVINGS

Neutral-flavored oil or cooking
  spray
1½ cups all-purpose flour
2 teaspoons baking powder
½ teaspoon kosher salt
6 large eggs
1½ cups milk
¾ cup cottage cheese
1 cup shredded Monterey Jack
  or Mexican cheese blend
2 (4-ounce) cans fire-roasted
  diced green chiles (mild
  variety), drained

A casserole with all of the rich and cheesy flavor of chiles rellenos, minus the effort it takes to stuff and fry the chiles. The preparation of this dish is a one-bowl affair—just whisk everything together, then pour it into a Pyrex dish and bake. It makes a nice brunch dish because it's got that eggy, cheesy thing going on, and it's also great for lunch and dinner. Serve it on its own or with Salsa Ranchera (page 274) or hot sauce on the side.

Preheat the oven on **BAKE** at 300°F and set the cooking time for 1 hour and 10 minutes. Lightly grease an 8-inch square Pyrex baking dish with oil or cooking spray.

In a mixing bowl, whisk together the flour, baking powder, and salt. Add the eggs and milk and whisk until thoroughly combined. Stir in the cottage cheese, Jack cheese, and green chiles. Pour the mixture into the greased baking dish. Place the baking dish on top of the cooking pan.

Bake the casserole in the preheated oven.

When the cooking program ends, wearing heat-resistant mitts, remove the baking dish from the oven. Let the casserole cool for 10 minutes—it will deflate a bit as it cools. Cut it into slices and serve warm.

Nutrition Information: Per serving: 356 calories, 14 grams fat, 37 grams carbohydrates, 1 gram fiber, 19 grams protein

GREEN FALAFEL SANDWICHES with CREAMY TAHINA

VEGAN, GLUTEN-FREE (make sure the oat flour is GF and serve without flatbreads or use GF flatbreads)

PREP TIME: 10 MINUTES, PLUS
24 HOURS TO SOAK THE CHICKPEAS

COOK TIME: 15 MINUTES

YIELD: 24 SMALL FALAFEL BALLS
(4 SERVINGS)

1 cup plus 1 tablespoon
    (8 ounces) dried chickpeas,
    soaked for 24 hours, water
    changed once halfway
    through soaking, drained,
    and rinsed

1 small yellow onion (4 ounces),
    diced

2 cloves garlic, pressed or
    minced

2 loosely packed cups coarsely
    chopped fresh cilantro
    (2 ounces, from a 3-ounce
    bunch, stems removed)

2 tablespoons oat flour or
    all-purpose flour

1 teaspoon ground coriander

1 teaspoon kosher salt

½ teaspoon ground cumin

¼ teaspoon ground black
    pepper

Pinch cayenne pepper

Olive oil, for spraying

4 flatbreads (page 292),
    warmed, for serving

1 batch Creamy Tahina
    (page 286), for serving

Two things are nontraditional about these falafels: They have a bit of oat flour to help them hold together, and of course they are air fried rather than deep-fried. The crispy little balls get a big punch of fresh herbal flavor from lots of cilantro. Tuck falafel into flatbreads (page 292) and serve them with Creamy Tahina (page 286), a tahini-based sauce, drizzled on top.

Combine the chickpeas, onion, garlic, cilantro, flour, coriander, salt, cumin, black pepper, and cayenne in a food processor. Process in 15 (1-second) pulses, until the chickpeas are finely chopped and the mixture resembles coarse, wet sand.

Place the air frying basket on top of a quarter sheet pan and spray the basket lightly with oil. Use a 1½-tablespoon cookie scoop to portion the mixture into balls, gently shaping each one into a ball or football shape with your hands before placing it in the basket. (Alternatively, if you don't mind flat-bottomed falafel balls, you can just scoop them right out into the basket.) Spray the falafel balls lightly with oil.

Place the black enamel cooking pan in the bottom oven rack position. Place the wire metal oven rack in the second highest position.

Preheat the oven on **AIR FRY** at 375°F and set the cooking time for 15 minutes.

recipe continues

NOTES

To dress up your falafel sandwiches with more toppings, look to the list on page 175 for inspiration.

To make larger falafel balls, use 3-tablespoon cookie scoop and air fry for an additional 5 minutes. The recipe will make about 14 larger balls.

Twenty-four hours may sound like a long time to soak chickpeas, but since they're ground up and fried straight from their soaked form rather than being boiled, I find that this gives the best texture to the finished dish.

Air fry the falafel in the preheated oven.

When the cooking program ends, transfer the falafel balls to flatbreads on serving plates. Drizzle with the tahini sauce and serve.

Nutrition Information: Per serving (6 falafel balls): 206 calories, 5 grams fat, 28 grams carbohydrates, 6 grams fiber, 12 grams protein

VARIATION **RED FALAFEL** Use half as much cilantro, and add 2 tablespoons harissa paste to the food processor.

CHIPOTLE MUSHROOM and POBLANO TACOS

DIETARY INFORMATION: VEGAN,
GLUTEN-FREE (use corn tortillas)

PREP TIME: 5 MINUTES
COOK TIME: 15 MINUTES
YIELD: 4 LARGE TACOS
(2 SERVINGS)

1 chipotle chile en adobo (from a can), minced (see note)

1½ tablespoons olive oil

1 clove garlic, pressed or minced

½ teaspoon chili powder

½ teaspoon kosher salt

¼ teaspoon dried oregano

½ pound cremini, oyster, or shiitake mushrooms, cut into ¼-inch slices

1 poblano chile, seeded and cut into ½×2-inch strips

4 taco-size corn or flour tortillas, warmed

FOR SERVING

¼ cup Avocado Crema (page 276) or store-bought crema Mexicana

2 tablespoons chopped fresh cilantro

Lime wedges

NOTE

Chipotles in adobo vary in their level of heat and can pack quite a punch! Use half of 1 chile rather than a whole one for less heat, or substitute ½ teaspoon smoked paprika for the chipotle.

Mushrooms and strips of poblano chile are roasted in a flavorful and smoky chipotle marinade. When roasted, the mushrooms become chewy and flavorful, contrasting with the soft and sweet poblano. Serve these tacos to vegetarians or omnivores—the flavors and textures will please any palate.

Preheat the oven on **ROAST** at 375°F and set the cooking time for 15 minutes. Line the cooking pan with parchment paper.

In a small bowl, stir together the chipotle, olive oil, garlic, chili powder, salt, and oregano. Add the mushrooms and poblano strips to a large mixing bowl. Pour in the chipotle mixture, then use your hands to toss, until the vegetables are evenly coated. Spread out the vegetables in an even layer on the lined cooking pan.

Roast the vegetables in the preheated oven. When the "**turn food**" message comes on, stir the vegetables, then return them to the oven.

When the cooking program ends, assemble and serve the tacos: Place the warmed tortillas on serving plates, then top each one with ⅓ cup of the roasted mushrooms and peppers. Top with avocado crema and cilantro. Serve with lime wedges alongside.

Nutrition Information: Per serving (2 tacos): 347 calories, 16 grams fat, 41 grams carbohydrates, 6 grams fiber, 9 grams protein

WHITE PIZZA with MUSHROOMS and ROSEMARY

VEGETARIAN

PREP TIME: 20 MINUTES
COOK TIME: 12 MINUTES
YIELD: 1 (12-INCH) PIZZA (8 SLICES)

1 cup shredded mozzarella cheese

½ cup whole-milk ricotta cheese

¼ cup grated parmesan cheese, plus more for serving

2 cloves garlic, chopped

About ¾ teaspoon chopped fresh rosemary leaves (from a 6-inch sprig)

¼ teaspoon kosher salt

4 ounces cremini mushrooms, sliced

2 teaspoons olive oil

⅛ teaspoon truffle salt

Flour, for the work surface

½ batch Refrigerator Pizza Dough (page 295) or 1 (1-pound) package store-bought pizza dough

Aleppo or regular red pepper flakes, for serving

The cremini mushrooms on top of this pizza are seasoned with truffle salt for even more mushroom flavor, and the three-cheese topping is fragrant with rosemary and garlic. Serve your pizza with a dinner salad, or pile some lightly dressed arugula on top just before slicing for a one-pan meal.

Line the cooking pan with parchment paper.

In a bowl, combine the mozzarella, ricotta, parmesan, garlic, rosemary, and kosher salt. Stir until evenly mixed. In another bowl, toss the mushrooms with the oil and truffle salt.

Liberally flour a work surface, then use a rolling pin and your hands to roll and stretch the pizza dough until it is a circle 11 inches in diameter and does not shrink back. (For the easiest time rolling the dough, I like to alternate between stretching the dough in my hands and rolling it on the countertop a few times.) Transfer the dough to the lined cooking pan.

Select the **BAKE** program at 400°F and set the cooking time for 12 minutes.

Spread out the cheese mixture on the pizza dough, leaving a ½-inch border around the edge. Sprinkle the mushrooms in an even layer on top of the cheese.

recipe continues

NOTES
The 12-minute bake time yields a well-browned pizza with good browning on the underside of the crust. If you prefer a more lightly browned pizza, reduce the baking time to 10 minutes.

Bake the pizza in the preheated oven.

When the cooking program ends, carefully slide the pizza and parchment onto a cutting board. Slice the pizza into 8 wedges and serve right away, with parmesan and pepper flakes on the side for sprinkling.

Nutrition Information: Per slice: 197 calories, 6 grams fat, 25 grams carbohydrates, 1 gram fiber, 11 grams protein

VARIATION You can use the same dough recipe (page 295), basic method, and baking time to make any pizza you like. For a basic pie, spread ½ cup marinara sauce (page 282) or store-bought pizza sauce over the dough, then top with 1 cup shredded mozzarella and whatever other toppings you prefer.

GRILLED CHEESE SANDWICHES

VEGAN/DAIRY-FREE (substitute vegan sliced cheese for the dairy cheese and use vegan mayonnaise, page 276)

GLUTEN-FREE (use GF sandwich bread)

PREP TIME: 5 MINUTES

COOK TIME: 8 MINUTES

YIELD: 1 SANDWICH

2 slices sandwich bread (sourdough, white, or whole-wheat)

1 tablespoon unsalted butter or mayonnaise (page 276)

2 ounces melting cheese (see note)

2 teaspoons grated parmesan cheese (optional)

I love the consistent results I get when making grilled cheese in the air fryer oven. It's always crunchy on the outside and melty on the inside, as it should be! Depending on the size of the bread, you can fit up to 4 sandwiches in the air frying basket at once, so feel free to scale up the recipe as needed. Butter is the classic choice for spreading on the outside of the bread, or you can spread on mayonnaise instead for a little extra tang. To add a special final touch, sprinkle a little parmesan on top of the sandwich during the last few minutes of cooking for a crispy, extra cheesy topping.

Place the black enamel cooking pan in the bottom oven rack position. Place the wire metal oven rack in the second highest position.

Preheat the oven on **AIR FRY** at 350°F and set the cooking time for 8 minutes.

Spread both pieces of bread with the butter or mayonnaise. Place 1 slice of bread, buttered side down, in the air frying basket, then top with the cheese and the second slice of bread, buttered side up.

Air fry the sandwich in the preheated oven. When the "**turn food**" message comes on, use a thin flexible spatula to flip the sandwich. Sprinkle the parmesan on top (if using), then return it to the oven.

recipe continues

If you'd like to lighten up your grilled cheese, spray the bread lightly with olive oil instead of using butter or mayo. You can also use less cheese, if you like.

Melting cheeses include cheddar, American, Havarti, mozzarella, Fontina, Muenster, Monterey Jack, Colby, or even pepper Jack for a little spicy kick.

When the cooking program ends, transfer the sandwich to a serving plate, cut in half diagonally, and serve.

Nutrition Information: Per sandwich: 500 calories, 31 grams fat, 34 grams carbohydrates, 2 grams fiber, 20 grams protein

VARIATION   GRILLED GRUYÈRE, ARUGULA, AND RED PEPPER Spread the outside of the bread with butter and the inside of the bread with 1 tablespoon mayo (page 276) or aioli. For the filling, layer 2 (1-ounce) slices Gruyère or swiss cheese, 2 tablespoons Mama Lil's hot peppers or chopped roasted red peppers, and ½ cup baby arugula.

TEMPEH IN TAMARIND SAUCE with KALE COCONUT SALAD

VEGAN, GLUTEN-FREE

PREP TIME: 15 MINUTES
COOK TIME: 15 MINUTES
YIELD: 4 SERVINGS

SALAD

1 bunch curly or lacinato kale, stems removed, cut into ¼-inch ribbons

½ cup unsweetened shredded coconut

2 tablespoons fresh lime juice

1 tablespoon avocado oil or other neutral-flavored oil

¼ teaspoon kosher salt

1 tablespoon agave nectar

1 large ripe mango, peeled, seeded, and diced

SAUCE

1 cup water

2 tablespoons tamarind paste

1 tablespoon sambal oelek or sriracha sauce

3 (¼-inch-thick) rounds ginger root, smashed

3 (2-inch-long) pieces lemongrass (white part of 1 stalk), smashed

¼ cup brown sugar

1 tablespoon avocado oil or other neutral-flavored oil

2 cloves garlic, sliced thinly

TEMPEH

2 (8-ounce) packages tempeh

2 tablespoons avocado oil or other neutral-flavored oil

2 shallots, sliced thinly

3 cups freshly cooked rice, for serving

When I lived in Santa Cruz in my college days, my favorite restaurant was Malabar, a Sri Lankan spot that made the most incredible vegan food. This recipe is loosely inspired by a dish they used to serve called Tempeh La La. In my version, pieces of tempeh are air fried until they are crisp and golden, then combined with shallots and a tangy and sweet tamarind sauce. Serve the tempeh with cooked rice and a raw kale salad for a satisfying vegan meal.

Make the salad: In a large bowl, combine the kale, coconut, lime juice, oil, and salt. Use your hands to squeeze and mix the salad for about 2 minutes, until the kale is very wilted. Add the agave nectar and mango and toss until evenly mixed. Set aside.

Make the sauce: In a bowl, stir together the water, tamarind paste, sambal, ginger, lemongrass, and sugar.

Heat the oil in a medium (3-quart) saucepan on the stove over medium heat or in an Instant Pot on its **SAUTE** program. Add the garlic and sauté for about 2 minutes, until the garlic is lightly toasted.

Add the tamarind mixture to the saucepan, then turn up the heat to medium-high. Bring the sauce up to a boil, then let it boil and reduce, stirring occasionally, until it is syrupy and about half its original volume, about 15 minutes. Turn off the heat, then use a fork or slotted spoon to remove all of the pieces of lemongrass and ginger from the pan.

While the sauce is reducing, prepare the tempeh: Cut the pieces of tempeh into 1-inch strips, then slice the strips crosswise into ⅓-inch-thick pieces.

Place the black enamel cooking pan in the bottom oven rack position. Place the wire metal oven rack in the second highest position.

Preheat the oven on **AIR FRY** at 360°F and set the cooking time for 15 minutes.

In a large mixing bowl, toss the tempeh with the oil until all of the pieces are evenly coated. Spread out the tempeh in an even layer in the air frying basket.

Add the shallots to the bowl and toss them in the residual oil, using your fingers to break them up into individual rings.

Air fry the tempeh in the preheated oven.

When the "**turn food**" message comes on, sprinkle the shallots over the tempeh in an even layer, then return the tempeh to the oven.

When the cooking program ends, transfer the tempeh and shallots to the saucepan with the sauce. Toss to coat evenly.

Spoon the tempeh and sauce onto serving plates and serve with the rice and salad alongside.

Nutrition Information: Per serving (tempeh and salad): 527 calories, 26 grams fat, 48 grams carbohydrates, 12 grams fiber, 26 grams protein

SESAME-SOY TOFU RICE BOWLS

VEGAN, GLUTEN-FREE (substitute GF tamari for the soy sauce)

PREP TIME: 5 MINUTES, PLUS 15 MINUTES TO PRESS THE TOFU AND 30 MINUTES TO MARINATE

COOK TIME: 12 MINUTES

YIELD: 4 SERVINGS

1 (14-ounce) block firm tofu

¼ cup soy sauce

¼ cup mirin (sweet cooking rice wine)

1 tablespoon avocado oil or other neutral-flavored oil

1 teaspoon toasted sesame oil

1 tablespoon cornstarch

3 cups cooked rice or other grain, for serving

4 cups roasted vegetables (page 216), for serving

1 teaspoon toasted sesame seeds, for garnish

1 green onion, sliced, for garnish

My mom has been baking tofu for decades, ever since my brother declared himself a vegan in high school. In my air fryer oven version, bite-size pieces of tofu are marinated for 30 minutes, then baked in just 12 minutes. The secret ingredient is a little bit of cornstarch, tossed with the tofu just before baking—it helps the tofu to crisp and brown around the edges. Serve the tofu on a rice bowl, as shown here, or on its own for snacking.

Drain the block of tofu. Place it in a tofu press, or place it on a dish and put a cast-iron or other heavy pan on top. Let sit for 15 minutes. Drain off the excess water that has collected, then pat the tofu dry with a paper towel. Cut the tofu into ¾-inch cubes and place it in a lidded container.

In a small bowl, stir together the soy sauce, mirin, avocado oil, and sesame oil. Pour the mixture over the tofu. Cover the tofu and marinate in the refrigerator for at least 30 minutes or up to overnight.

Preheat the oven on **BAKE** at 375°F and set the cooking time for 12 minutes. Line the cooking pan with parchment paper.

Use a slotted spoon to transfer the tofu to a mixing bowl. Reserve the marinade. Sprinkle the cornstarch over the tofu, then use a spatula to toss gently, coating the tofu pieces with the cornstarch without breaking them up. Spread out the tofu in an even layer on the lined cooking pan.

recipe continues

Bake the tofu in the preheated oven.

While the tofu is baking, assemble the rice bowls: In each bowl, place ¾ cup of the rice and 1 cup of the roasted vegetables.

When the cooking program ends, use a spatula to transfer the tofu to the rice bowls. Top the tofu with the reserved marinade, sesame seeds, and green onions, and serve.

Nutrition Information: Per serving (tofu and marinade only): 185 calories, 8 grams fat, 16 grams carbohydrates, 1 gram fiber, 11 grams protein (Nutrition info per rice bowl varies based on ingredients used.)

CHICK'N NUGGETS with HONEY BBQ SAUCE

VEGAN (substitute agave syrup for honey)

GLUTEN-FREE (substitute GF tamari for the soy sauce, GF flour blend for the all-purpose flour, and GF panko bread crumbs for the regular panko)

PREP TIME: 10 MINUTES, PLUS 15 MINUTES TO PRESS THE TOFU AND 15 MINUTES TO MARINATE

COOK TIME: 20 MINUTES

YIELD: 4 SERVINGS

1 (14-ounce) block extra firm tofu

MARINADE

2 tablespoons soy sauce

1 tablespoon plus 1 teaspoon apple cider vinegar

1 tablespoon olive oil

1 tablespoon nutritional yeast

½ teaspoon garlic powder

½ teaspoon onion powder

½ teaspoon poultry seasoning (page 289)

Pinch cayenne pepper

BATTER

½ cup all-purpose flour

½ cup plant-based milk

1 tablespoon olive oil

¼ teaspoon ground black pepper

¼ teaspoon kosher salt

1¼ cups panko bread crumbs

Avocado oil or other neutral-flavored oil, for spraying

¼ cup barbecue sauce (page 280)

1 tablespoon honey or agave nectar

Crispy on the outside, soft and tender on the inside, and dipped in a sweet barbecue sauce. These are everything you want out of a chicken nugget, minus the chicken! Look to the dietary information for vegan and gluten-free substitutions.

Drain the block of tofu. Place it in a tofu press, or place it on a dish and put a cast-iron or other heavy pan on top. Let sit for 15 minutes. Drain off the excess water that has collected, then pat the tofu dry with a paper towel. Cut the tofu into 1-inch cubes.

Marinate the tofu: In a large mixing bowl, stir together the soy sauce, vinegar, oil, nutritional yeast, garlic powder, onion powder, poultry seasoning, and cayenne. Add the tofu and use a spatula to toss gently, coating the tofu pieces with the marinade without breaking them up. Let marinate for at least 15 minutes or up to overnight in the fridge.

Make the batter: In another mixing bowl, whisk together the flour, milk, oil, black pepper, and salt until no lumps remain. Add the tofu and toss gently so all of the pieces are coated in the batter.

recipe continues

NOTE

Instead of the barbecue
sauce, you can also pair
these with honey mustard
sauce (page 284), ketchup
(page 279), or sweet chili garlic
sauce (page 285) for dipping.

Place the bread crumbs in a shallow bowl. Line the air frying
basket with parchment paper and spray it lightly with oil.

Use a pair of forks to transfer a tofu nugget from the batter to
the bowl of bread crumbs. Lightly coat the nugget with bread
crumbs on all sides, then place it in the air frying basket. Repeat
with the remaining nuggets, making sure not to let them touch,
or they will stick together as they cook.

Place the black enamel cooking pan in the bottom oven rack position. Place the wire metal oven rack in the second highest position.

Preheat the oven on **AIR FRY** at 375°F and set the cooking time
for 20 minutes.

Spray the nuggets lightly with oil.

Air fry the nuggets in the preheated oven. When the "**turn food**"
message comes on, use tongs to flip the nuggets, then return
them to the oven.

While the nuggets are finishing cooking, stir together the barbecue sauce and honey in a small bowl.

When the cooking program ends, transfer the nuggets to a serving platter or plates. Serve with the sauce on the side.

Nutrition Information: Per serving (nuggets only): 286 calories, 12 grams fat,
29 grams carbohydrates, 3 grams fiber, 14 grams protein

CRISPY MASALA CHICKPEA SALAD BOWLS

VEGAN, GLUTEN-FREE

PREP TIME: 5 MINUTES
COOK TIME: 12 MINUTES
YIELD: 4 SERVINGS

CHICKPEAS

1½ cups cooked chickpeas (from a 15-ounce can or homemade), drained

2 teaspoons olive oil

2 teaspoons chaat masala, or 1 teaspoon garam masala plus ½ teaspoon kosher salt

TAMARIND DRESSING

¼ cup avocado oil or other neutral-flavored oil

3 tablespoons rice vinegar

1 tablespoon tamarind concentrate

1 tablespoon granulated sugar

2 tablespoons chopped fresh cilantro

1 clove garlic, chopped

¾ teaspoon kosher salt

Pinch cayenne pepper

SALAD

8 cups spring mix

1 large avocado, pitted, peeled, and cubed

2 Persian cucumbers, sliced

1 navel orange, peeled and sliced into supremes

½ cup cherry or grape tomatoes, halved

¼ cup currants, raisins, or dried cranberries

¼ cup roasted pepitas (shelled pumpkin seeds) or sunflower seeds

This recipe is inspired by the salads at Zareen's, a Pakistani/Indian restaurant in Palo Alto, California. Their Orange Is the New Green salad is a delightful and inventive mix of Indian flavors and California ingredients, with a tangy tamarind dressing drizzled on top. I've added crispy roasted chickpeas flavored with chaat masala, a spice blend available online and at Indian grocery stores.

Place the black enamel cooking pan in the bottom oven rack position. Place the wire metal oven rack in the second highest position.

Preheat the oven on **AIR FRY** at 400°F and set the cooking time for 8 minutes.

In a mixing bowl, toss the chickpeas in the olive oil. Spread out the chickpeas in the air frying basket.

Air fry the chickpeas in the preheated oven. When the "**turn food**" message comes on, wearing heat-resistant mitts, give them a quick shake, then return them to the oven.

recipe continues

If you do not have tamarind concentrate, you can substitute 1 tablespoon pomegranate molasses or 1 tablespoon lemon juice plus 1 tablespoon brown sugar. The flavor will be slightly different but still good.

These chickpeas are crispy on the outside, with soft centers. For very dry, extra-crispy chickpeas, increase the cooking time to 12 minutes.

While the chickpeas are cooking, make the dressing: In a blender, combine the avocado oil, vinegar, tamarind concentrate, sugar, cilantro, garlic, salt, and cayenne. Blend at medium speed for about 30 seconds, until smooth.

When the cooking program ends, transfer the chickpeas back to the mixing bowl, sprinkle the chaat masala over them, and toss to coat evenly.

Assemble the salads: In bowls or on plates, arrange the spring mix, avocado, cucumbers, oranges, tomatoes, currants, and pepitas. Add the chickpeas, then spoon the dressing over the salads. Serve right away.

Nutrition Information: Per serving: 427 calories, 27 grams fat, 36 grams carbohydrates, 10 grams fiber, 12 grams protein

CHAPTER 4

BEEF & PORK

MARINATED TRI-TIP ROAST and BROCCOLI SALAD

GLUTEN-FREE (substitute GF tamari or aminos for the soy sauce)

DAIRY-FREE

PREP TIME: 10 MINUTES, PLUS 6 HOURS TO MARINATE AND 15 MINUTES TO REST

COOK TIME: 35 TO 45 MINUTES, DEPENDING ON DONENESS

YIELD: 8 SERVINGS

MARINATED TRI-TIP ROAST

2 tablespoons balsamic vinegar

2 tablespoons soy sauce

1 tablespoon fish sauce, or another tablespoon soy sauce

1 tablespoon olive oil

1 teaspoon kosher salt

1 teaspoon ground black pepper

1 teaspoon garlic powder

1 teaspoon smoked paprika

1 (2½-pound) tri-tip roast

BROCCOLI SALAD

½ cup mayonnaise (page 276)

1 tablespoon Dijon mustard

2 tablespoons apple cider vinegar

2 tablespoons granulated sugar

1 teaspoon kosher salt

4 large stalks broccoli, florets separated, stems peeled and julienned (about 6 cups total)

2 large carrots, peeled and julienned (about 1½ cups)

1 small red onion, diced small (about 1 cup)

1 cup raw whole cashews, toasted in a dry skillet for 5 minutes, cooled, and coarsely chopped

½ cup raisins

Tri-tip roasts benefit from a long marinade—if you can marinate it the day before you cook it, you will be rewarded with well-seasoned, tender meat. Balsamic vinegar adds a bit of sweetness and helps to create a beautifully charred surface on the meat as it roasts. While the meat roasts, you'll make a crunchy, creamy broccoli salad. Once the tri-tip is out of the oven and resting, you can roast some potatoes (page 237) to serve alongside.

Marinate the roast: In a large shallow dish or a jar lined with a 1-gallon ziplock bag, combine the vinegar, soy sauce, fish sauce, olive oil, salt, pepper, garlic powder, and paprika. Stir until evenly mixed. Add the tri-tip roast to the marinade, flipping it a few times to coat it evenly. Cover the dish or close the bag and marinate the roast in the refrigerator for at least 6 hours or up to overnight.

Preheat the oven on **ROAST** at 360°F and set the cooking time for 35 minutes for medium-rare to medium, 40 minutes for medium to medium-well, or 45 minutes for well-done. Line the cooking pan with aluminum foil or parchment paper.

Remove the roast from the marinade and pat the roast dry with paper towels. Discard the marinade. Place the roast on the lined cooking pan.

Due to the irregular shape of a tri-tip roast, you'll end up with a variety of donenesses—it will be more well-done on the thinner end, while the thickest part will end up rarest, with the lowest internal temperature. This is actually an advantage if you're serving a group with a variety of preferences.

Tri-tip roasts can vary in thickness and weight. Additionally, the internal temperature of the roast when you put it in the oven will affect the cooking time. The given times are for fairly thick, 2½-pound roast, cooked straight from the refrigerator. A good rule of thumb is 14 minutes per pound for medium to medium-rare, 16 minutes per pound for medium to medium-well, and 18 minutes per pound for well-done. Go by the reading of the probe thermometer for the most accurate results.

This marinade also works well for other cuts of steak, such as London broil and flank.

Roast the tri-tip in the preheated oven.

While the tri-tip is roasting, make the salad: In a salad bowl, whisk together the mayonnaise, mustard, vinegar, sugar, and salt. Add the broccoli, carrot, onion, cashews, and raisins, and toss to combine. Refrigerate the salad until you are ready to serve. Toss it once more just before serving.

When the cooking program ends, use an instant-read thermometer to check the internal temperature of the thickest part of the roast to make sure it has reached the desired level of doneness. The internal temperature of the meat will rise about 15°F as it rests, so for medium-rare to medium, for instance, you'll want to stop the cooking when the internal temperature reaches 120°F, as it will rise to about 135°F as it rests. Refer to the Temperature Chart for Steak (see page 138) to determine the desired temperature. If the temperature is lower than you want it, cook the roast for a few more minutes, then test again.

Transfer the cooked roast to a carving board and let it rest for 15 minutes. Cut the roast in half crosswise, then carve it into ¼-inch-thick slices against the grain. Serve warm, with some juices from the carving board spooned on top and the salad alongside.

Nutrition Information: Per serving of tri-tip: 262 calories, 15 grams fat, 1 gram carbohydrates, 0 grams fiber, 30 grams protein

Per serving of salad: 259 calories, 17 grams fat, 21 grams carbohydrates, 5 grams fiber, 11 grams sugar, 6 grams protein

RIB-EYE or STRIP STEAKS with HERB BUTTER

**GLUTEN-FREE, DAIRY-FREE
(substitute 1 tablespoon olive oil for
the butter)**

PREP TIME: 5 MINUTES, PLUS
5 MINUTES TO REST
COOK TIME: 12 MINUTES
YIELD: 4 SERVINGS

HERB BUTTER

2 tablespoons unsalted butter,
  room temperature
1 tablespoon chopped fresh
  parsley
½ teaspoon chopped fresh
  rosemary leaves
⅛ teaspoon salt
Pinch ground black pepper

STEAK

½ teaspoon paprika
½ teaspoon garlic powder
¼ teaspoon ground black
  pepper
1 teaspoon kosher salt
2 (12-ounce) boneless rib-eye
  or strip steaks (1⅜ to 1½
  inches thick)
Avocado oil, for spraying

A good steak is a special occasion food, so you want to get it just right. Using your air fryer oven ensures consistent results, so you'll get evenly seared, properly cooked steaks every time. Pats of herb butter melt over the steaks as they rest, giving extra richness to every bite.

Make the herb butter: In a small bowl, combine the butter, parsley, rosemary, salt, and pepper. Use a fork to mash and mix until well combined. Set aside.

Place the black enamel cooking pan in the bottom oven rack position. Place the wire metal oven rack in the second highest position.

Preheat the oven on **AIR FRY** at 400°F and set the cooking time for 12 minutes for rare steak, 15 minutes for medium, or 17 minutes for medium-well.

Season and cook the steaks: In another small bowl, mix up the paprika, garlic powder, pepper, and salt. Pat the steaks dry with paper towels. Sprinkle the seasoning mixture evenly over both sides of the steaks, spray the steaks lightly on both sides with oil, and place them in the air frying basket.

Air fry the steaks in the preheated oven. When the **"turn food"** message comes on, use tongs to flip the steaks onto their second side, then return them to the oven.

recipe continues

NOTE
You can cook other cuts of steak this way, too, including top sirloin, T-bone, skirt steak, flank steak, and filet mignon. Depending on their thickness, different cuts will take different amounts of time. For thinner steaks, start taking the internal temperature after 8 minutes of cooking time to ensure that they end up at the desired level of doneness. For thicker, bone-in steaks, reduce the cooking temperature to 375°F.

When the cooking program ends, use an instant-read thermometer to check the internal temperature of the middle of each steak to make sure they have reached the desired level of doneness. The internal temperature of the meat will rise about 7°F as it rests, so for rare steak, for instance, you'll want to stop the cooking when the internal temperature reaches 113°F to 118°F, as it will rise to 120°F to 125°F as it rests. Refer to the Temperature Chart for Steak (see below) to determine the desired temperature. If the temperature is lower than you want it, cook the steaks for a few more minutes, then test again.

When the steaks are done to your preference, transfer to a carving board and allow to rest for 5 minutes. Carve the steaks into ½-inch-thick slices, transfer to serving plates, top with the herb butter, and serve right away.

Nutrition Information: Per 6-ounce serving of USDA Choice rib-eye steak, with butter: 368 calories, 25 grams fat, 3 grams carbohydrates, 0 grams fiber, 33 grams protein

TEMPERATURE CHART FOR STEAK
Rare: 120°F to 125°F
Medium-rare: 130°F to 135°F
Medium: 140°F to 145°F
Medium-well: 150°F to 155°F
Well-done: 160°F+

CHICKEN-FRIED STEAK and COUNTRY GRAVY

DAIRY-FREE (substitute unsweetened plant-based milk for milk)

PREP TIME: 15 MINUTES
COOK TIME: 10 MINUTES
YIELD: 4 SERVINGS

STEAK

2 (8-ounce) steaks (strip steak or top sirloin works well; see note)

BREADING

1 cup all-purpose flour

1 teaspoon garlic powder

2 teaspoons seasoned salt (page 291)

½ teaspoon ground black pepper

2 large eggs

2 tablespoons water

Avocado oil or other neutral-flavored oil, for spraying

COUNTRY GRAVY

2 tablespoons unsalted butter

2 tablespoons all-purpose flour

½ cup chicken stock

¾ cup milk

½ teaspoon kosher salt

½ teaspoon ground black pepper

A classic comfort dish with a confusing name, this is steak, breaded and fried in the style of Southern-fried chicken. The steak is pounded into a thin paillard before it's dredged in seasoned flour and beaten eggs, and it cooks in just 10 minutes. While the steak cooks, you'll whisk up a creamy country gravy. Serve with a simple side of roasted vegetables (page 216) for a healthier take on this diner favorite.

Prepare the steaks: Cut the steaks in half to make 4 (4-ounce) portions. Place 1 piece of steak between 2 sheets of plastic wrap and use a meat tenderizing mallet to pound it out to a ⅓- to ½-inch-thick paillard. Repeat with the remaining portions. Pat the steaks dry with paper towels.

Create a breading station with a quarter sheet pan and a shallow bowl: In the quarter sheet pan, stir together the flour, garlic powder, seasoned salt, and pepper until evenly mixed. In the shallow bowl, whisk the eggs and water until no streaks remain.

Dredge a piece of steak in the flour, then shake any excess flour back into the bowl. Next, dip the steak in the egg mixture, holding it over the bowl for a few seconds to let any excess egg drip back into the bowl. Next, place the steak back in the flour. Coat all sides evenly, flipping it and pressing in the flour a few times to make sure the steak is very dry and floury on the outside, with none of the egg wash peeking through. Place the steak in the corner of

recipe continues

My favorite steak to use for this recipe is strip steak, trimmed of any excess fat and gristle. I buy them in value packs when they're on sale, then trim and freeze them for later use. Top sirloin is also very good. You can also use cube steaks, straight out of the package, with no trimming or pounding required.

the quarter sheet pan, sitting on top of the flour. Repeat with the remaining steaks, leaving them all in the pan of flour, making sure not to overlap them.

While the steaks are still in the pan of flour, spray their tops lightly with oil, taking care to moisten any dry floury spots.

Place the black enamel cooking pan in the bottom oven rack position to catch any drips. Place the wire metal oven rack in the second highest position.

Preheat the oven on **AIR FRY** at 400°F and set the cooking time for 10 minutes.

When the oven is preheated, transfer the steaks from the pan of flour to the air fryer basket, and place it in the oven immediately. When the "**turn food**" message comes on, use a thin flexible spatula to flip the steaks. Spray their second sides lightly with oil, then return them to the oven.

While the steaks are cooking, make the gravy: In a 1½-quart saucepan, melt the butter over medium heat. Add the flour and cook for about 2 minutes, stirring often, until it is blond but not browned. While whisking, slowly pour in the chicken stock, then the milk, and add the salt and pepper. Bring the gravy up to a simmer, stirring often, and let simmer for about 1 minute, until thickened. Remove from heat and cover until the steaks are done.

When the cooking program ends, transfer the steaks to serving plates. Ladle gravy over the top of each steak and serve.

Nutrition Information: Per serving (1 steak and ⅓ cup gravy): 356 calories, 18 grams fat, 19 grams carbohydrates, 1 gram fiber, 28 grams protein

KOREAN-STYLE SHORT RIBS (Kalbi)

GLUTEN-FREE (substitute GF tamari
for the soy sauce)
DAIRY-FREE

PREP TIME: 10 MINUTES, PLUS
1 HOUR TO MARINATE
COOK TIME: 10 MINUTES
YIELD: 4 SERVINGS

1 pound flanken-style (thin
   cross-cut) short ribs

MARINADE

2 tablespoons soy sauce

2 tablespoons water

2 tablespoons brown sugar

1 tablespoon mirin (sweet
   cooking rice wine)

1½ teaspoons toasted
   sesame oil

½ teaspoon ground black
   pepper

1 kiwi or ½ pear, peeled and
   quartered

2 cloves garlic, peeled

1 green onion, sliced thinly, for
   garnish

3 cups cooked rice, for serving

1 head butter lettuce,
   separated into leaves and
   washed, for serving

Korean-Style Dipping Sauce
   (page 281), for serving

One of the first places my husband and I grabbed dinner when we moved to Portland was 808 Grinds, a Hawaiian food cart parked next to Gigantic Brewery. Enjoying a pint and an order of their delicious kalbi, I was inspired to make my own version. Kalbi refers to a cut of meat (short ribs) as well as a style of preparation—they're traditionally marinated, then grilled over charcoal. These baked short ribs are an easier alternative to grilling, and they take just 10 minutes to cook through. Serve them as an appetizer with dipping sauce (page 281), rice, and lettuce leaves for wrapping.

Rinse the ribs under running water to remove any bits of bone. Pat the ribs with paper towels, then place them in a large shallow dish or ziplock bag.

Make the marinade: In a blender, combine the soy sauce, water, sugar, mirin, oil, pepper, kiwi, and garlic. Blend at high speed for about 30 seconds until smooth.

Pour the marinade over the ribs, flipping them a few times so they are all coated evenly. Cover the dish or close the bag and marinate in the refrigerator for at least 1 hour or up to overnight.

Preheat the oven on **BAKE** at 400°F and set the cooking time for 10 minutes. Line the cooking pan with aluminum foil.

Shake off the excess marinade from the ribs, then place them on the lined cooking pan in a single layer. Discard any remaining marinade.

Bake the ribs in the preheated oven. When the **"turn food"** message comes on, use tongs to flip the ribs onto their second side, then return them to the oven.

When the cooking program ends, transfer the ribs to serving plates and sprinkle the green onion on top. Serve right away, with rice, lettuce leaves, and dipping sauce alongside.

Nutrition Information: Per serving (ribs only): 300 calories, 22 grams fat, 5 grams carbohydrates, 0 grams fiber, 20 grams protein

QUARTER-POUNDER HAMBURGERS

GLUTEN-FREE (use GF hamburger buns)
DAIRY-FREE (omit the cheese)

PREP TIME: 10 MINUTES
COOK TIME: 9 MINUTES
YIELD: 4 BURGERS

1 pound ground beef
   (90% lean or whatever
   percentage you prefer)
¾ teaspoon kosher salt
¼ teaspoon ground black
   pepper
¼ cup mayonnaise (page 276)
3 tablespoons ketchup
   (page 279)
1 tablespoon yellow mustard
½ dill pickle, minced, or
   2 tablespoons dill pickle
   relish
4 slices cheddar or American
   cheese (optional)
4 hamburger buns
½ dill pickle, sliced thinly
1 beefsteak or similar slicing
   tomato, sliced thinly
2 large leaves iceberg or
   butter lettuce

Yep, you can cook hamburgers in the air fryer oven! Air frying them in the basket helps to keep the mess to a minimum, since any drippings are directed downward to the cooking pan rather than onto the sides of the oven. For me, this beats cleaning up my stovetop, hands down. And the burgers come out juicy on the inside, with a well-browned exterior, every time.

Shape the ground beef into 4 (4-ounce) burgers, each 3½ inches in diameter. Make a 1-inch-wide divot in the center of each burger. (This will help to keep them flat when cooking.) Season the burgers with the salt and pepper and place them in the air frying basket.

Place the black enamel cooking pan in the bottom oven rack position. Place the air frying basket on top of the wire metal oven rack in the second highest position.

Select the **BROIL** program at 400°F and set the cooking time for 9 minutes for medium-rare burgers, 10 minutes for medium, or 11 minutes for medium-well.

Broil the burgers. After 5 minutes have passed, use a thin flexible spatula to flip the burgers, then return them to the oven.

While the burgers are cooking, mix up the mayonnaise, ketchup, mustard, and minced pickle in a small bowl.

When the cooking program ends, wearing heat-resistant mitts, remove the air frying basket with the burgers and the cooking

recipe continues

NOTE

You can cook frozen burgers in the air fryer oven this way, too. Air fry frozen ⅓-pound burgers for 15 minutes at 350°F.

pan from the oven. Use a paper towel to wipe the wire oven rack to avoid any grease dripping onto the heating elements. If you're using cheese, put a slice on top of each burger.

Place the wire oven rack in the oven in the second-highest position. Select **TOAST** at Level 1 for 4 slices, and toast the buns.

When the buns are toasted, assemble the burgers: Spread about 1 tablespoon of the burger sauce on each half of the buns. Place a burger on each bottom bun and a few pickle slices on each top bun. On top of each burger, place slices of tomato and ½ lettuce leaf. Place the top buns on the burgers and serve right away.

Nutrition Information: Per serving (without cheese): 403 calories, 16 grams fat, 32 grams carbohydrates, 2 grams fiber, 28 grams protein

ITALIAN-STYLE MEATBALLS MARINARA

GLUTEN-FREE (substitute GF bread for the French bread and GF pasta for wheat pasta)

DAIRY-FREE (substitute plant-based milk for the dairy milk and omit the cheese)

PREP TIME: 10 MINUTES

COOK TIME: 15 MINUTES

YIELD: 4 SERVINGS

Kosher salt

2 slices (3 ounces) French or Italian bread, cubed (about 2½ cups)

½ cup milk or any unsweetened plant-based milk

1 pound ground beef (90% lean)

1 large egg

2 cloves garlic, pressed or grated on a fine Microplane

½ cup grated parmesan cheese (optional)

1 teaspoon Italian seasoning

½ teaspoon salt

¼ teaspoon ground black pepper

8 ounces dried spaghetti

1 batch Roasted Marinara Sauce (page 282), or 2 cups your favorite store-bought pasta sauce

1 tablespoon chopped fresh parsley, for garnish

Generously sized, juicy meatballs bake in just 15 minutes in the air fryer oven. I use a 3-tablespoon cookie scoop to portion them easily and quickly, and I don't bother to roll them into perfect spheres—flat-bottomed meatballs are fine by me. Put some water on to boil the pasta before you start the recipe, heat the sauce when the pasta goes in the water, and everything will be ready at the same time.

Bring a large pot of salted water to a boil.

Place the cubed bread in a large mixing bowl. Pour the milk over the bread and let the milk soak into the bread for 5 minutes. Add the beef, egg, garlic, ¼ cup of the cheese (if using), Italian seasoning, ½ teaspoon salt (or ¾ teaspoon if leaving out the cheese), and the pepper. Use your hands to mix until evenly combined—it's fine if there are some visible bits of bread throughout.

Preheat the oven on **BAKE** at 350°F and set the cooking time for 15 minutes. Line the cooking pan with foil.

Use a 3-tablespoon cookie scoop to portion out 12 meatballs onto the lined pan.

Bake the meatballs in the preheated oven.

While the meatballs are baking, cook the spaghetti according to package directions, then drain. Heat the marinara sauce in a small saucepan over medium heat.

recipe continues

When the cooking program ends, wearing heat-resistant mitts, remove the meatballs from the oven. Serve them over the spaghetti, with marinara sauce, parsley, and the remaining ¼ cup parmesan (if you like) on top.

Nutrition Information: Per serving (meatballs, sauce, and pasta, without cheese): 573 calories, 21 grams fat, 58 grams carbohydrates, 5 grams fiber, 35 grams protein

VARIATION   SUBMARINE SANDWICHES You can also serve these meatballs in submarine sandwiches with peppers and onions (page 231). Prepare the peppers and onions, then the meatballs. Place hoagie or submarine sandwich rolls cut side up on the cooking pan. Layer on the peppers and onions, then the meatballs. Ladle on marinara sauce, top with provolone or mozzarella cheese, and **TOAST** at Level 2 for 4 slices until the cheese is bubbling and lightly browned.

BISON MEATLOAF MEATBALLS

GLUTEN-FREE (use GF oats)
DAIRY-FREE (use plant-based milk)

PREP TIME: 10 MINUTES
COOK TIME: 18 MINUTES
YIELD: 4 SERVINGS

BISON MEATBALLS

1 pound ground bison or beef
(90% lean)

¼ large sweet yellow onion,
finely diced (¾ cup)

½ cup old-fashioned oats

⅓ cup milk (dairy or
unsweetened plant-based)

1 large egg

2 cloves garlic, pressed or
minced

1 teaspoon Worcestershire
sauce

½ teaspoon Italian seasoning

½ teaspoon ground black
pepper

½ teaspoon kosher salt

¼ teaspoon red chile flakes

MEATLOAF GLAZE

⅓ cup ketchup (page 279)

2 teaspoons yellow mustard

2 tablespoons brown sugar

¼ teaspoon Tabasco sauce or
other hot sauce

NOTE

If you like, you can substitute
barbecue sauce (page 280) for
the glaze.

These ultra-savory, fast-cooking meatballs are inspired by the meatloaf served at the now-closed Delessio Market in San Francisco, one of my favorite lunch spots when I was in grad school at the nearby conservatory. Using oats as a binder gave their meatloaf an extra hearty texture that kept me and my classmates coming back for more. For a side dish, I usually make some Instant Pot mashed potatoes while the meatballs are baking or heat up some leftover roasted veggies (page 216).

Make the meatballs: In a large mixing bowl, combine bison, onion, oats, milk, egg, garlic, Worcestershire, Italian seasoning, black pepper, salt, and red chile flakes. Use your hands to mix until evenly combined.

Make the glaze: In a small bowl, mix together the ketchup, mustard, sugar, and Tabasco.

Preheat the oven on **BAKE** at 350°F and set the cooking time for 18 minutes. Line the cooking pan with parchment paper or aluminum foil.

Use a 3-tablespoon cookie scoop to portion out the meatballs onto the cooking pan. Spoon 2 teaspoons of the glaze on top of each meatball.

Bake the meatballs in the preheated oven.

When the cooking program ends, transfer the meatballs to serving plates and serve.

Nutrition Information: Per serving: 320 calories, 13 grams fat, 22 grams carbohydrates, 1 gram fiber, 26 grams protein

GLAZED QUARTER-HAM

GLUTEN-FREE, DAIRY-FREE
(substitute vegan butter for the butter)

PREP TIME: 5 MINUTES
COOK TIME: 50 MINUTES
YIELD: 4 SERVINGS

1 (2-pound) boneless quarter-ham (sliced or unsliced)

¼ cup maple syrup

1 tablespoon brown sugar

1 tablespoon unsalted butter

Pinch ground cloves

Pinch cayenne pepper (optional)

I love to serve a quarter-ham for a small holiday get-together or a cozy dinner anytime. These past 2 years, we've celebrated Easter with only our immediate family, and I was glad to be able to purchase a ham on the smaller side! They come fully cooked, presliced, and basically ready to go. All you have to do is wrap the ham in foil, bring it up to serving temperature on your oven's **ROAST** program, then coat the ham with a sweet and subtly spiced maple syrup glaze.

Preheat the oven on **ROAST** at 350°F and set the cooking time for 45 minutes. Line the cooking pan with aluminum foil.

Place the ham on another sheet of foil. Bring the foil up around the sides of the ham and crimp the foil shut at the top, so the ham is fully enclosed. Place it on the cooking pan.

Roast the ham in the preheated oven.

While the ham roasts, make the glaze on the stovetop: In a small saucepan over medium heat, combine the maple syrup, sugar, butter, cloves, and cayenne (if using). When the mixture comes up to a simmer, turn the heat down to low. Let simmer for about 5 minutes, stirring occasionally, until the glaze is slightly thickened. Remove from the heat.

When the cooking program ends, wearing heat-resistant mitts, remove the ham from the oven.

recipe continues

NOTES

Quarter-hams can vary in size—the ones at my local grocery stores weigh in at around 2 pounds, and that's what I've used here. If you are cooking a larger ham, factor in an additional 15 minutes per pound of roasting time before removing the foil.

This method also works well with a "sweetheart ham," a cured and smoked product made from the pork sirloin tip that weighs 2 to 3 pounds. Olympia Provisions sells a wonderful one.

Unwrap the ham, taking care not to get burned by the steam or juices that may have accumulated under the foil. (Use an instant-read thermometer to check the temperature of the ham—it should be at least 140°F in the middle. If not, rewrap and roast the ham for a few more minutes, until it has come up to temperature.)

Preheat the oven once again on **ROAST** at 375°F and set the cooking time for 5 minutes.

Check the glaze: If it has solidified, return it to medium heat for a minute or so, until it is warm and pourable. Pour the glaze over the ham.

Roast the ham in the preheated oven for the final 5 minutes.

Wearing heat-resistant mitts, remove the ham from the oven. If it's not already sliced, transfer it to a carving board and slice with a carving knife or chef's knife. Transfer slices to a serving platter or plates and serve warm.

Nutrition Information: Per serving: 227 calories, 6 grams fat, 24 grams carbohydrates, 0 grams fiber, 20 grams protein

ROTISSERIE RUBBED PORK TENDERLOIN and POTATOES

GLUTEN-FREE, DAIRY-FREE

PREP TIME: 10 MINUTES, PLUS
10 MINUTES TO REST

COOK TIME: 30 MINUTES

YIELD: 4 SERVINGS

1½ pounds petite gold or red
    potatoes

1½ teaspoons olive oil

½ teaspoon seasoned salt
    (page 291)

3 tablespoons barbecue rub
    (page 288)

1 (1¼-pound) pork tenderloin

Pork tenderloin is my favorite meat to cook on the rotisserie spit. It comes out so tender and evenly browned, and there's room to roast some potatoes underneath. Coat the tenderloin with barbecue rub (page 288), or use your favorite store-bought seasoning blend for an even easier dinner. The rubs from Meat Church and Traeger are very good.

Line the cooking pan with aluminum foil. In a large mixing bowl, toss the potatoes with the oil and seasoned salt. Arrange the potatoes around the perimeter of the pan.

Sprinkle the rub evenly over the pork tenderloin, coating it on all sides. Thread it onto the rotisserie spit, then screw on the rotisserie forks, adjusting them so that the tenderloin is firmly anchored in the center of the spit.

Place the cooking pan in the oven in the lowest rack position. Place the pointed end of the rotisserie spit in its catch on the right side of the oven, then lower the squared-off end of the spit into its notch on the left side of the oven. Check to make sure that the potatoes are out of the way of the roast, so they will not hinder the rotation of the spit.

Select the **ROAST** program at 375°F and set the cooking time for 30 minutes. Make sure the **"Rotate"** function is on and the rotisserie spit is rotating.

recipe continues

When the cooking program ends, wearing heat-resistant mitts, use the rotisserie lift to remove the spit from the oven. Transfer the tenderloin, still on the spit, to a carving board. Let the tenderloin rest for 10 minutes. Unscrew and remove the rotisserie forks. Remove the spit from the tenderloin. Cut the pork into ½-inch-thick slices and serve with the potatoes alongside.

Nutrition Information: Per serving (meat and potatoes): 318 calories, 6 grams fat, 34 grams carbohydrates, 4 grams fiber, 31 grams protein

TWO-HOUR BBQ BABY BACK RIBS with CLASSIC COLESLAW

GLUTEN-FREE, DAIRY-FREE

PREP TIME: 10 MINUTES
COOK TIME: 1 HOUR 40 MINUTES
YIELD: 4 SERVINGS

RIBS

1 (2½- to 3-pound) rack pork baby back ribs

2 tablespoons barbecue rub (page 288)

¼ cup your favorite barbecue sauce (I like Stubb's), plus more for serving

CLASSIC COLESLAW

3 tablespoons mayonnaise (page 276)

1 teaspoon Dijon mustard

1 teaspoon apple cider vinegar

1 teaspoon granulated sugar

¼ teaspoon kosher salt

¼ teaspoon ground black pepper

½ medium head green cabbage, shredded (about 4 cups)

1 medium carrot, peeled and grated

½ small yellow onion, minced

2 tablespoons chopped fresh parsley

Dinner in 2 hours might sound like a long time, but since so much of it is unattended, these ribs really are as easy as it gets. They are seasoned with a homemade barbecue rub, then glazed with your store-bought sauce of choice. While the ribs cook, toss together the coleslaw. And if you like, serve some dinner rolls or prepare a batch of garlic bread (page 75) to toast once the ribs are out of the oven.

Line the cooking pan with aluminum foil.

Make the ribs: Use a paring knife to cut under a corner of the silverskin (the tough membrane on the bony side of the rack of ribs). Use a paper towel to grip the corner of the silverskin, then pull it away and discard. Cut the rack of ribs into 4 (3-rib) sections, then place on the lined pan.

Sprinkle the rub all over the ribs, turn them meat side up, then cover the pan tightly with aluminum foil. (At this point, you can cook the ribs right away or refrigerate up to overnight.)

Preheat the oven on **BAKE** at 300°F and set the cooking time for 1 hour and 30 minutes.

Bake the ribs in the preheated oven.

While the ribs cook, make the coleslaw: In a salad bowl, whisk together the mayonnaise, mustard, vinegar, sugar, salt, and

recipe continues

pepper. Add the cabbage, carrot, onion, and parsley and toss to combine. Cover and refrigerate the coleslaw until you are ready to serve, tossing it once more just before serving.

When the cooking program ends, wearing heat-resistant mitts, remove the cooking pan from the oven and remove the foil cover, taking care not to get burned by the steam or to slosh the cooking liquid out of the pan.

Preheat the oven on **BAKE** at 375°F and set the cooking time for 10 minutes.

Brush the top of each rib section with 1 tablespoon of the barbecue sauce.

Bake the ribs in the preheated oven, uncovered. The barbecue sauce will set into a glaze.

Using tongs, transfer the ribs to serving plates. Serve with the coleslaw alongside and more barbecue sauce for dipping.

Nutrition Information: Per serving of ribs: 282 calories, 18 grams fat, 7 grams carbohydrates, 1 gram fiber, 21 grams protein

Per serving of coleslaw: 81 calories, 3 grams fat, 12 grams carbohydrates, 7 grams fiber, 3 grams protein

PORK BELLY BITES

GLUTEN-FREE, DAIRY-FREE

PREP TIME: 5 MINUTES, PLUS
15 MINUTES TO REST
COOK TIME: 1 HOUR 45 MINUTES
YIELD: 8 SERVINGS

2 pound slab pork belly (about
1¼ inches thick), skin
removed

2 tablespoons barbecue rub
(page 288)

1 cup barbecue sauce
(page 280), for serving

Pork belly bites are one of my husband Brendan's favorite dishes. You can serve them as a main dish or an appetizer—a little goes a long way since they are so rich. Sprinkled with barbecue rub (page 288), then slowly baked, the pork stays juicy and tender, while the long cooking time allows much of the fat to render out. Serve the bites with barbecue sauce (page 280) on the side for dipping.

Preheat the oven on **BAKE** at 300°F and set the cooking time for 1 hour and 45 minutes. Line the cooking pan with aluminum foil.

Season the pork belly on both sides with the rub, then use your hands to rub it in to coat the pork evenly. Place the pork on the lined cooking pan fat side up.

Bake the pork in the preheated oven.

When the program ends, wearing heat-resistant mitts, remove the pork from the oven. Transfer the pork to a carving board and allow it to rest for 15 minutes. Use a carving knife or chef's knife to cut it into ¾-inch squares. Serve warm, with barbecue sauce on the side.

Nutrition Information: Per serving (bites with barbecue sauce): 290 calories, 22.5 grams fat, 21 grams carbohydrates, 0 grams fiber, 27 grams protein

PORK RIND–CRUSTED PORK CHOPS

GLUTEN-FREE, DAIRY-FREE

PREP TIME: 15 MINUTES, PLUS
2 HOURS TO BRINE
COOK TIME: 12 MINUTES
YIELD: 4 SERVINGS

BRINE

2 cups water

3 tablespoons kosher salt

2 tablespoons honey or maple
syrup

½ teaspoon red pepper flakes

1 sprig fresh rosemary, 3 sprigs
fresh thyme, or ½ teaspoon
dried rosemary or thyme

2 cloves garlic, smashed, or
½ teaspoon garlic powder

3 cups ice cubes

4 (½-inch-thick) boneless
pork loin chops (1⅓ pounds
total)

2 large eggs

2 teaspoons medium-spicy
hot sauce such as Frank's
RedHot (optional)

1 cup pork rind breading
(page 294)

Brined pork chops are very forgiving to cook—they're guaranteed to be well-seasoned through and through, and they stay juicy even when cooked well-done. The brine takes just 10 minutes to make, and you can let the pork chops brine for as little as 2 hours. As for the breading, it's a highly seasoned, keto-friendly blend of pork rinds and almond flour. Look to the note for timing and temperature for cooking pork chops without a breading.

Make the brine: Combine the water, salt, honey, red pepper flakes, rosemary, and garlic in a medium saucepan over medium-high heat, or in an Instant Pot on the **SAUTE** program. Stir often until the salt is dissolved and the brine begins to simmer, about 5 minutes. Remove the pot from the heat and add the ice cubes. Allow the ice to melt completely, stirring a couple times, about 3 minutes.

Place the pork chops in a 2-quart baking dish or a gallon ziplock bag and cover them with the brine. Cover the baking dish or close the bag and refrigerate for at least 2 hours or up to 8 hours.

Line the air fryer tray with parchment paper. Place the black enamel cooking pan in the bottom oven rack position to catch any drips. Place the wire metal oven rack in the second highest position.

Pat the pork chops dry with paper towels. Discard the brine.

recipe continues

Create a breading station with two shallow bowls: In the first bowl, whisk the eggs and hot sauce until no streaks remain. Add the breading to the second bowl.

Dredge a pork chop in the egg mixture, holding it over the bowl for a few seconds to let any excess egg drip back into the bowl. Next, place the pork chop in the bowl of breading and flip it to coat on both sides. Transfer the pork chop to the air frying basket. Repeat with the remaining pork chops.

Preheat the oven on **AIR FRY** at 375°F and set the cooking time for 12 minutes.

Air fry the pork chops in the preheated oven. When the "**turn food**" message comes on, use a thin flexible spatula to flip the pork chops, being careful not to remove any of the breading, then return them to the oven.

When the cooking program ends, transfer the pork chops to serving plates and serve.

Nutrition Information: Per serving: 255 calories, 12 grams fat, 3 grams carbohydrates, 1 gram fiber, 36 grams protein

GOCHUJANG-SPICED PORK MEATBALLS with CUCUMBER SALAD

PREP TIME: 10 MINUTES
COOK TIME: 10 MINUTES
YIELD: 4 SERVINGS

PORK MEATBALLS

1 pound ground pork
    (90% lean)

1 large egg

½ cup panko bread crumbs

2 tablespoons gochujang

2 teaspoons toasted sesame oil

3 cloves garlic, pressed or
    minced

½-inch piece ginger root,
    finely grated, or ½ teaspoon
    ground ginger

½ teaspoon kosher salt

CUCUMBER SALAD

1 English cucumber, sliced into
    thin rounds

2 tablespoons rice vinegar

1 tablespoon granulated sugar

¼ teaspoon kosher salt

3 cups cooked rice or
    cauliflower rice, for serving

2 teaspoons sesame seeds,
    for garnish

This dish borrows ingredients from Korea and Japan—gochujang gives the meatballs a sweet heat, while the accompanying cucumbers get a dressing of rice vinegar, making for a pickled salad similar to sunomono. Serve the meatballs and cucumbers over rice or cauliflower rice for a fast and flavorful dinner—one of my favorites to make on weeknights when I need to throw together a last-minute meal.

Line the cooking pan with parchment paper or aluminum foil.

Make the meatballs: In a large mixing bowl, use your hands to combine the pork, egg, bread crumbs, gochujang, sesame oil, garlic, ginger, and salt.

Preheat the oven on **BAKE** at 375°F and set the cooking time for 10 minutes.

Use a 1½-tablespoon cookie scoop to portion the meatball mixture into 20 meatballs onto the lined baking pan.

Bake the meatballs in the preheated oven. While the meatballs are baking, make the cucumber salad: In a mixing bowl, combine the cucumbers, vinegar, sugar, and salt.

When the cooking program ends, transfer the meatballs to serving bowls with the rice and cucumbers. Sprinkle with sesame seeds and serve right away.

Nutrition Information: Per serving (meatballs and salad): 313 calories, 15 grams fat, 16 grams carbohydrates, 1 gram fiber, 26 grams protein

CHAPTER 5

CHICKEN & TURKEY

ROTISSERIE or ROASTED WHOLE CHICKEN

GLUTEN-FREE, DAIRY-FREE

PREP TIME: 10 MINUTES, PLUS
15 MINUTES TO REST

COOK TIME: 40 MINUTES

YIELD: 1 CHICKEN (4 TO 6
SERVINGS)

1 (3-pound) whole chicken
(see the variation for
roasting a larger bird)

1½ teaspoons seasoned salt
(page 291)

2 teaspoons avocado oil or
other neutral-flavored oil

This is the simplest chicken you're ever going to cook! Season the bird with seasoned salt, rub in the spices with a little bit of oil, then rotisserie or roast it until the skin is browned and the meat is juicy and tender. While the chicken is resting on the carving board, roast some potatoes (page 237) or vegetables (page 216) to serve alongside.

Line the cooking pan with aluminum foil.

Truss the chicken: Place the chicken breast side up on a cutting board. Thread a 3-foot piece of butcher's twine underneath the chicken. Pick up the twine from both ends, letting it catch just behind the wings. Bring the twine up and around the sides of the chicken, pinning down the wings against the breast, then cross the two ends underneath the tip of the breast.

Next, bring the ends of the twine up and around the ends of the drumsticks, so they are pinned against each other. Holding the twine in place, turn the chicken over onto its back. Bring the ends of the twine around the tail, tighten, and tie in a firm double knot. Trim the ends of the twine.

Thread the chicken onto the rotisserie spit, then screw on the rotisserie forks, adjusting them so that the chicken is firmly anchored in the center of the spit.

Sprinkle the seasoned salt evenly over the chicken. Drizzle the oil over the chicken, then use your hands to rub it in evenly.

Place the cooking pan in the oven in the lowest rack position. Place the pointed end of the rotisserie spit in its catch on the right side

of the oven, then lower the squared-off end of the spit into its notch on the left side of the oven.

Select the **ROAST** program at 380°F and set the cooking time for 40 minutes. Check to make sure the "**Rotate**" function is on and the rotisserie spit is rotating.

When the cooking program ends, use an instant-read thermometer to check the internal temperature of the chicken at the thickest part of the breast and thigh—the breast should register at least

recipe continues

The rotisserie spit in the Omni Plus air fryer oven has a maximum weight limit of 4 pounds, but I have found that most 4-pound chickens are too large to fit unless they are extremely tightly trussed, and even then it can be a snug fit. The smaller chickens from Cooks Venture, available online and in some markets, are my favorites to cook on the rotisserie.

When roasting larger chickens, you may find that the fat drippings begin to create white smoke after the chicken has been cooking for a while. You can pour off the excess drippings periodically, if you like, and make sure to ventilate your kitchen well.

165°F, and the thigh should register 170°F or higher. If it is not yet up to temperature, roast for a few more minutes, then test again.

Use the rotisserie lift to remove the spit from the oven. Transfer the chicken, still on the spit, to a carving board. Let the chicken rest for 15 minutes.

Unscrew and remove the rotisserie forks. Remove the spit from the chicken. Carve the chicken into quarters and serve.

Nutrition Information: Per 3-ounce portion (meat with skin, off the bone): 140 calories, 7 grams fat, 1 gram carbohydrates, 0 grams fiber, 19 grams protein

VARIATION ROASTING INSTRUCTIONS FOR CHICKENS LARGER THAN 3 POUNDS Season and truss the chicken as written above, using ½ teaspoon seasoned salt and ½ teaspoon oil per pound. Line the cooking pan with foil, then place a sheet of parchment paper on top of the foil (this will prevent the chicken from sticking). Place the chicken on the lined cooking pan, breast side down. Place the chicken in the oven, then select the **ROAST** program at 380°F with a cook time of 15 minutes per pound. (For chickens larger than 4½ pounds, reduce the cooking temperature to 350°F.) Check to make sure the "**Rotate**" function is off. When the "**turn food**" message comes on, wearing heat-resistant mitts, use tongs to flip the chicken breast side up, then return it to the oven. When the cooking program ends, use an instant-read thermometer to check the chicken for doneness; cook for additional time if it has not reached 165°F. Rest, carve, and serve the chicken as in the main recipe.

JERK-SPICED CHICKEN with MANGO SALSA

GLUTEN-FREE (substitute GF tamari for the soy sauce)
DAIRY-FREE

PREP TIME: 10 MINUTES, PLUS
8 HOURS TO MARINATE
COOK TIME: 45 MINUTES
YIELD: 6 SERVINGS

3 pounds bone-in skin-on chicken (drumsticks, thighs, leg quarters, or half breasts, cut in half crosswise)

JERK MARINADE

4 green onions, cut into 1-inch pieces

3 cloves garlic, peeled

2 habanero chiles, stemmed and seeded

3 tablespoons fresh lime juice (from 1 lime)

2 tablespoons olive oil

2 tablespoons soy sauce

1 teaspoon kosher salt

1 tablespoon brown sugar

1 teaspoon ground allspice

1 teaspoon ground black pepper

½ teaspoon dried thyme

½ teaspoon smoked paprika

¼ teaspoon ground nutmeg

¼ teaspoon ground cinnamon

MANGO SALSA

1 large mango, peeled, pitted, and diced

¼ medium sweet onion, diced

1 serrano chile, seeded and minced

2 teaspoons chopped fresh cilantro

1 tablespoon fresh lime juice

1 teaspoon brown sugar

¼ teaspoon kosher salt

In the early days of our relationship, dates for my husband and me often included takeout from Back-A-Yard, our favorite Caribbean restaurant in Menlo Park, California. Now that we live in another state, I make my own version whenever we are in the mood for spicy, well-seasoned chicken. Habaneros are much easier to find than the traditional Scotch bonnet peppers, and they add a similar kick of heat to the marinade.

Place the chicken pieces in a large shallow dish or 1-gallon ziplock bag.

Make the marinade: Combine green onions, garlic, chiles, lime juice, oil, soy sauce, salt, sugar, allspice, pepper, thyme, paprika, nutmeg, and cinnamon in a blender. Blend at medium speed for 30 seconds, until well blended.

Pour the marinade over the chicken and toss the pieces to coat evenly. Cover the dish or close the bag and refrigerate for at least 8 hours or up to 24 hours. (A 24-hour marinade results in much more flavorful chicken.)

recipe continues

Take the chicken out of the fridge 1 hour before you want to cook it. Line the cooking pan with foil, and place a wire cooling rack on the lined pan.

Preheat the oven on **BAKE** at 325°F and set the cooking time for 45 minutes.

Shake off any excess marinade from the chicken, then place the pieces skin side up on the cooling rack. Discard the marinade.

Bake the chicken in the preheated oven.

While the chicken is cooking, make the salsa: In a bowl, stir together the mango, onion, chile, cilantro, lime juice, sugar, and salt.

When the cooking program ends, use an instant-read thermometer to check the internal temperature of the chicken pieces at their thickest parts, without touching the bone—breasts should register at least 165°F, and legs and thighs should register 170°F or higher (I prefer them at 185°F). If the chicken is not yet up to temperature, bake for a few more minutes, then test again. (If some pieces are done sooner than others, remove them and continue to cook the rest of the chicken.)

Transfer the chicken pieces to a serving platter or plates. Let rest for 10 minutes. Serve with the salsa on the side.

Nutrition Information: Per serving (two drumsticks and salsa): 406 calories, 21 grams fat, 8.5 grams carbohydrates, 2 grams fiber, 45 grams protein

CRISPY AIR-FRIED CHICKEN with SRIRACHA-HONEY DRIZZLE

PREP TIME: 15 MINUTES, PLUS
2 HOURS TO MARINATE
COOK TIME: 30 MINUTES
YIELD: 6 SERVINGS

CHICKEN

1 cup buttermilk

¼ cup Frank's RedHot sauce

2 pounds bone-in skin-on chicken (drumsticks, thighs, wings, and/or breasts cut in half crosswise)

1¼ cups all-purpose flour

1 teaspoon garlic powder

2 teaspoons seasoned salt (page 291)

1 teaspoon poultry seasoning (page 289)

¼ teaspoon cayenne pepper

Avocado oil or other neutral-flavored oil, for spraying

SRIRACHA-HONEY DRIZZLE

¼ cup clover or wildflower honey

¼ cup sriracha sauce

Air-fried chicken tastes just as good as deep-fried chicken, with so much less oil. It's one of my favorite things to make in the air fryer because the payoff is so great. You get crispy pieces of chicken that are delicious straight out of the oven and even better when they're drizzled with sweet and spicy sriracha. Serve with coleslaw (page 157) or broccoli salad (page 134).

Marinate the chicken: In a large shallow dish or 1-gallon ziplock bag, combine the buttermilk and hot sauce. Add the chicken, flipping it to coat completely. Cover the dish or close the bag and refrigerate for at least 2 hours or up to overnight.

Line a baking sheet or large dish with parchment paper. (This is where you'll place the breaded pieces of chicken before air frying—if they sit too long in the air frying basket before cooking, the breading will stick to the metal.)

Create a breading station with two shallow bowls: In the first bowl, stir together the flour, garlic powder, seasoned salt, poultry seasoning, and cayenne until evenly mixed. Drain the buttermilk marinade from the chicken into the second bowl.

Pat the chicken pieces dry with paper towels. One at a time, dredge the chicken pieces in the flour mixture, then the buttermilk marinade, then back in the flour for a second time. Place the coated pieces skin side up on the lined baking sheet.

recipe continues

VARIATION You can substitute 1 pound boneless thighs or breast tenders for the bone-in chicken. Air fry the breaded pieces at 400°F for 15 minutes. Pair boneless fried chicken with Classic Coleslaw (page 157) to make sandwiches on hamburger buns or kaiser rolls.

Place the black enamel cooking pan in the bottom oven rack position to catch any drips. Place the wire metal oven rack in the second highest position.

Preheat the oven on **AIR FRY** at 350°F and set the cooking time for 30 minutes.

Spray the tops of the chicken pieces lightly with avocado oil, taking care to moisten the entire surface so it is no longer dry and floury. Right when the oven has preheated, transfer the breaded chicken to the air frying basket.

Air fry the chicken in the preheated oven. When the "**turn food**" message comes on, use tongs to flip the pieces of chicken. If there are any dry, floury spots on their second side, spray them lightly with oil, then return the basket to the oven.

While the chicken is cooking, make the drizzle: In a small bowl, stir together the honey and sriracha.

When the cooking program ends, use an instant-read thermometer to make sure the chicken is cooked through: 185°F in the center for thighs and drumsticks, 165°F for breasts.

Using tongs, transfer the chicken to serving plates. Drizzle the chicken with the sriracha honey or serve it on the side for dipping. Serve right away.

Nutrition Information: Per serving: 314 calories, 14 grams fat, 11 grams carbohydrates, 0 grams fiber, 32 grams protein

SHAWARMA-SPICED CHICKEN WRAPS

GLUTEN-FREE (use GF flatbread)

PREP TIME: 10 MINUTES
COOK TIME: 15 MINUTES
YIELD: 4 WRAPS

1¼ pounds boneless skinless chicken thighs

1 tablespoon shawarma spice blend (page 290)

2 teaspoons olive oil

2 cloves garlic, pressed or grated on a Microplane

4 flatbreads (page 292)

½ cup White Shawarma Sauce (page 278)

OPTIONAL TOPPINGS

Hot sauce (zhoug or your favorite)

Shredded lettuce

Pepperoncini

Sour or dill pickle slices

Diced cucumbers and tomatoes

Sliced red onion

Chopped cilantro

Ground sumac

I love the shawarma wraps served at casual restaurants in Israel—you're offered your choice from a huge selection of toppings to stuff into the flatbread along with tender spit-roasted meat. Authentic shawarma is cooked on a vertical rotating spit in enormous quantities, but if you want just a few servings at home, the air fryer oven is your best bet. Chop up the cooked chicken and serve it tucked into homemade flatbreads (page 292) with whatever toppings you like from the list below. Part of the fun is customizing your own wrap, so get creative and choose your favorite combination of creamy, crunchy, pickled, and spicy toppings.

Preheat the oven on **BAKE** at 400°F and set the cooking time for 15 minutes. Line the cooking pan with aluminum foil or parchment paper.

Place the chicken thighs on the cooking pan, spreading them out so you can see their whole surface. Sprinkle the spice blend, oil, and garlic over the chicken. Use your hands to rub the seasonings and oil all over the chicken thighs, and spread them out again—they will cook more evenly if they are not folded over but are in a single layer.

Bake the chicken thighs in the preheated oven. (While the chicken thighs are baking, you can prepare your optional toppings, choosing from the list given here.)

When the cooking program ends, use an instant-read thermometer to make sure the chicken is cooked through—the thighs should

recipe continues

NOTE
In my experience, especially thick boneless chicken thighs can take up to 18 minutes to cook through.

register at least 185°F in the center. If they are not yet up to temperature, bake for a few more minutes. Remove the chicken thighs from the oven and transfer them to a cutting board.

Place the flatbreads on the wire oven rack in the oven. Select **TOAST** at Level 1 for 1 slice.

While the flatbreads are toasting, chop the chicken thighs into bite-size pieces.

Transfer the toasted flatbreads to serving plates. Portion the chicken out onto the toasted flatbreads, add the shawarma sauce, and serve right away. Allow diners to choose whatever toppings they like.

Nutrition Information: Per serving (chicken, flatbread, and sauce): 481 calories, 28 grams fat, 31 grams carbohydrates, 2 grams fiber, 26 grams protein

PARMESAN CHICKEN TENDERS with HONEY MUSTARD SAUCE

GLUTEN-FREE (use GF flour blend and GF bread crumbs)
DAIRY-FREE (omit the parmesan)

PREP TIME: 10 MINUTES
COOK TIME: 8 MINUTES
YIELD: 4 SERVINGS

½ cup all-purpose flour

¼ teaspoon kosher salt

¼ teaspoon ground black pepper

¼ teaspoon garlic powder

2 large eggs

2 tablespoons water

1 cup panko or plain bread crumbs (page 296)

½ cup grated parmesan cheese

1 teaspoon Italian seasoning

1 pound chicken tenders

Olive oil, for spraying

1 batch Honey Mustard Dipping Sauce (page 284), for serving

Chicken tenders are kid friendly, and adults love them, too. With a crispy coating of bread crumbs and parmesan cheese and a honey mustard sauce for dunking, this version is irresistible. For an easy side salad, serve the tenders with a pile of mixed greens and cherry tomatoes that have been tossed in a little bit of the mustard sauce—it makes a good dressing, too.

Place the air frying basket on top of a quarter sheet pan. (This setup will help keep the floury mess to a minimum while you're breading the chicken—you won't be placing the quarter sheet pan in the oven.)

Create a breading station with three shallow bowls: In the first bowl, stir together the flour, salt, pepper, and garlic powder until evenly mixed. In the second bowl, whisk the eggs and water until no streaks remain. In the third bowl, stir together the bread crumbs, parmesan, and Italian seasoning until evenly mixed.

Dredge 1 chicken tender in the flour mixture, then shake any excess flour back into the bowl. Next, dip the chicken in the egg mixture, holding it over the bowl for a few seconds to let any excess egg drip back into the bowl. Finally, place the chicken in the bread crumb mixture and gently toss, making sure to coat all sides evenly. Transfer the breaded chicken tender to the air frying basket. Repeat with the remaining tenders.

recipe continues

Place the black enamel cooking pan in the bottom oven rack position to catch any drips. Place the wire metal oven rack in the second highest position.

Preheat the oven on **AIR FRY** at 400°F and set the cooking time for 8 minutes.

Spray the chicken tenders lightly with olive oil.

Air fry the chicken tenders in the preheated oven. When the **"turn food"** message comes on, use tongs to flip the tenders, then return them to the oven.

When the cooking program ends, use an instant-read thermometer to make sure that the tenders are cooked through. It should register 165°F when inserted into the thickest part.

Use tongs to transfer the tenders to serving plates. Serve with honey mustard sauce on the side.

Nutrition Information: Per serving (tenders only): 217 calories, 5 grams fat, 14 grams carbohydrates, 1 gram fiber, 27 grams protein

VARIATION For a low-carb and gluten-free version, substitute almond flour for the all-purpose flour and pork rind breading (page 294) for the parmesan–bread crumb mixture.

JAPANESE-STYLE CHICKEN CUTLETS (Katsu)

DAIRY-FREE

PREP TIME: 15 MINUTES
COOK TIME: 18 MINUTES
YIELD: 2 LARGE CUTLETS
(4 SERVINGS)

CHICKEN CUTLETS

2 boneless skinless chicken breasts (1 pound total; see note)

½ cup flour

1 large egg

2 teaspoons white miso

2 teaspoons water

1 cup panko bread crumbs

Avocado oil or other neutral-flavored oil, for spraying

KATSU SAUCE

2 tablespoons Worcestershire sauce

2 tablespoons ketchup (page 279)

½ teaspoon granulated sugar

1 teaspoon soy sauce

FOR SERVING

½ medium head green cabbage, shredded (about 4 cups)

½ cup sliced cherry tomatoes

3 cups cooked rice

Katsu is the Japanese term for breaded and fried cutlets. It's one of my favorite preparations for chicken breasts, which stay tender and juicy when they're pounded thin, covered in bread crumbs, and air fried. A little bit of miso in the egg wash gives them an extra savory flavor. Enjoy the cutlets sliced and served over rice, or look to the variation to make a katsu sandwich, as pictured on page 183.

Prepare the chicken: Sandwich each chicken breast between 2 sheets of plastic wrap. Use a meat mallet to pound out the breasts until they are about ½ inch thick.

Create a breading station with three shallow bowls: Add the flour to the first bowl. In the second bowl, whisk the egg, miso, and water until evenly combined and no streaks remain. Add the bread crumbs to the third bowl.

Line the air frying basket with parchment paper. Place the black enamel cooking pan in the bottom oven rack position to catch any drips. Place the wire metal oven rack in the second highest position.

Dredge 1 chicken cutlet in the flour, then shake any excess flour back into the bowl. Next, dip the cutlet in the egg mixture, holding it over the bowl for a few seconds to let any excess egg drip back into the bowl. Finally, place the cutlet in the bowl of bread crumbs,

recipe continues

Some boneless skinless chicken breasts can weigh 14 ounces or more. For those on the bigger side, you can butterfly them before pounding, then cut them in half to make 2 cutlets each.

flipping it and pressing down firmly a few times to make sure it is well coated. Transfer the breaded chicken cutlet to the lined air frying basket. Repeat with the remaining chicken breast.

Preheat the oven on **AIR FRY** at 350°F and set the cooking time for 18 minutes.

Spray the cutlet lightly with avocado oil.

Air fry the cutlets in the preheated oven. When the "**turn food**" message comes on, use tongs to flip the cutlets. Spray their second side with the oil, then return them to the oven.

While the cutlets are cooking, make the katsu sauce: In a small bowl, stir together the Worcestershire, ketchup, sugar, and soy sauce.

When the cooking program ends, transfer the chicken cutlets to a cutting board. Slice them into ¾-inch strips.

Transfer the chicken to serving plates, drizzle with katsu sauce, and serve with the shredded cabbage, cherry tomatoes, and rice alongside.

Nutrition Information: Per serving (½ cutlet and 1 tablespoon katsu sauce): 253 calories, 4 grams fat, 22 grams carbohydrates, 0 grams fiber, 29 grams protein

VARIATION · KATSU SANDWICH (AS PICTURED) Once the chicken cutlets are cooked, toast 2 sandwich rolls or 4 thick slices white bread on **TOAST** at Level 1 for 2 slices. Spread honey mustard sauce (page 284) on the toasted bread, then make sandwiches with shredded green cabbage, katsu sauce, chicken, and sliced tomatoes.

SLOW-COOKED CHICKEN with OLIVES and CAPERS

GLUTEN-FREE (use GF pasta)

DAIRY-FREE

PREP TIME: 5 MINUTES

COOK TIME: 2 HOURS

YIELD: 4 SERVINGS

1 cup marinara sauce (page 282) or other pasta sauce

½ large red onion, sliced thinly

½ cup pimiento-stuffed or plain pitted green olives

2 cloves garlic, pressed or chopped

2 tablespoons olive oil

1 teaspoon dried oregano

1 teaspoon capers, rinsed

1 pound boneless skinless chicken breasts (2 breasts)

8 ounces dried pasta such as spaghetti or linguine

Chicken breasts cook to fall-apart tenderness in a flavorful sauce with a base of marinara sauce (page 282 or store-bought) for a very easy meal. You'll use your air fryer oven's **SLOW COOK** or **BAKE** program at a low temperature for set-it-and-forget-it convenience. Olives and capers make this feel a lot fancier than most weeknight chicken dishes, and you can serve it over pasta, rice, farro, or even zucchini noodles for a lower-carb meal.

Add the marinara sauce, onion, olives, garlic, olive oil, oregano, and capers to an 8-inch square Pyrex baking dish. Toss to combine, then add the chicken and toss to coat evenly. Cover the dish tightly with aluminum foil.

Place the baking dish on top of the cooking pan and place it in the oven. Select **SLOW COOK** or **BAKE** at 210°F and set the cooking time for 2 hours.

When the chicken has been cooking for about 1 hour and 30 minutes, cook the pasta according to the package instructions. Drain it and keep it warm.

When the cooking program ends, wearing heat-resistant mitts, transfer the baking dish to a heat-resistant trivet. Carefully remove the foil, taking care not to get burned by the steam. Use a pair of forks to shred the chicken and mix it up with the sauce. Serve the chicken and sauce over the pasta.

Nutrition Information: Per serving (chicken, sauce, and pasta): 426 calories, 12 grams fat, 46 grams carbohydrates, 4 grams fiber, 31 grams protein

THANKSGIVING TURKEY THIGHS

GLUTEN-FREE, DAIRY-FREE
(substitute vegan butter or olive oil
for the butter)

PREP TIME: 10 MINUTES, PLUS
15 MINUTES TO REST

COOK TIME: 1 HOUR 15 MINUTES

YIELD: 6 SERVINGS

- 2 bone-in skin-on turkey thighs (1¼ pounds each)
- 2 tablespoons unsalted butter, room temperature
- 1 clove garlic, pressed or minced
- 1 teaspoon Dijon mustard
- 1 teaspoon poultry seasoning (page 289)
- 1 teaspoon sweet paprika
- 1 teaspoon kosher salt
- ½ teaspoon ground black pepper

If you're having a small Thanksgiving get-together or cozy fall dinner, there's no need to cook an entire turkey. Turkey thighs are big enough to serve at least two people each, their dark meat is rich and flavorful even without a brine or marinade, and they cook in a little over an hour. Look to the note for instructions to make some irresistible, crunchy croutons using the drippings.

Preheat the oven on **ROAST** at 300°F and set the cooking time for 1 hour and 15 minutes. Line the cooking pan with aluminum foil or parchment paper.

Pat the turkey thighs dry with paper towels, then place them on the lined cooking pan.

In a small bowl, combine the butter, garlic, mustard, poultry seasoning, paprika, salt, and pepper. Rub the butter mixture all over the turkey thighs.

Roast the turkey thighs in the preheated oven.

When the cooking program ends, check the internal temperature of the turkey thighs with an instant-read thermometer inserted into the thickest part without touching the bone. The turkey thighs are technically done when they have reached at least 165°F, but I actually prefer them between 180°F and 185°F, as they are a bit more tender. (If the turkey thighs aren't yet up to temperature but the skin is quite

For some wonderfully flavorful Thanksgiving croutons, cube 5 slices sourdough bread, then toss the bread cubes in the cooking fat and juices on the cooking pan. Roast at 375°F for 10 minutes. Sprinkle the croutons on salad, or use them as a crunchy topping for mashed potatoes or mac 'n cheese.

browned, you can tent them with foil, return them to the oven, and roast them for a few more minutes, until they are up to the desired temperature.)

Transfer the turkey thighs to a carving board and let rest for 15 minutes. Slice and serve.

Nutrition Information: Per 4-ounce serving (meat with skin, no bones): 205 calories, 8 grams fat, 0 grams carbohydrates, 0 grams fiber, 31 grams protein

JUICY TURKEY BURGERS

DAIRY-FREE (use DF burger buns or other bread)

PREP TIME: 5 MINUTES, PLUS
20 MINUTES TO REFRIGERATE
COOK TIME: 10 MINUTES
YIELD: 4 BURGERS

1 pound ground turkey (93% lean)

¼ cup plain bread crumbs (page 296)

¼ cup mayonnaise (page 276)

1 large egg

1 teaspoon Dijon mustard

1 teaspoon garlic powder

1 teaspoon sweet paprika

1 teaspoon poultry seasoning (page 289)

½ teaspoon kosher salt

¼ teaspoon ground black pepper

Avocado oil or other neutral-flavored oil, for spraying

4 hamburger buns

1 batch Burger Sauce (page 283)

1 beefsteak or similar slicing tomato, sliced thinly

4 leaves iceberg or butter lettuce

½ dill pickle, sliced thinly

My approach to making turkey burgers is completely different from beef burgers, since ground turkey tends to be dry and crumbly if it's cooked as is. Here, bread crumbs, mayonnaise, and egg are mixed in with the meat to keep the burgers nice and juicy. Serve them with the same fixings as hamburgers (page 145), or look to the variation for instructions on baking the mixture as meatballs instead.

In a mixing bowl, combine the ground turkey, bread crumbs, mayonnaise, egg, mustard, garlic powder, paprika, poultry seasoning, salt, and pepper. Use a spoon to mix until well combined. Cover the bowl and refrigerate for 20 minutes or up to overnight.

Preheat the oven on **BAKE** at 350°F and set the cooking time for 10 minutes. Line the cooking pan with parchment paper and spray it lightly with oil.

Shape the turkey into 4 (½-inch-thick) burgers on the lined cooking pan. Spray the burgers lightly with oil.

Bake the burgers in the preheated oven.

When the cooking program ends, remove the burgers from the oven.

Place the wire metal oven rack in the oven, then place the buns on the rack. Select **TOAST** at Level 1 for 2 slices and toast the buns.

When the buns are toasted, assemble the burgers: Spread about 2 tablespoons of the burger sauce on the top half of each hamburger bun. Place a burger on each bottom bun. On top of each burger, place slices of tomato, lettuce, and pickle. Place the top buns on the burgers and serve right away.

Nutrition Information: Per burger sandwich (burger, bun, sauce, tomato, lettuce, and pickles): 430 calories, 18 grams fat, 34 grams carbohydrates, 3 grams fiber, 29 grams protein

VARIATION · TURKEY MEATBALLS Once you've made and chilled the burger mixture, preheat the oven on **BAKE** at 350°F and set the cooking time for 15 minutes. Line the cooking pan with foil. Use a 3-tablespoon cookie scoop to portion out 12 meatballs onto the lined cooking pan. Bake the meatballs in the preheated oven. Serve with cooked pasta and marinara sauce (page 282) or in a submarine sandwich (page 148).

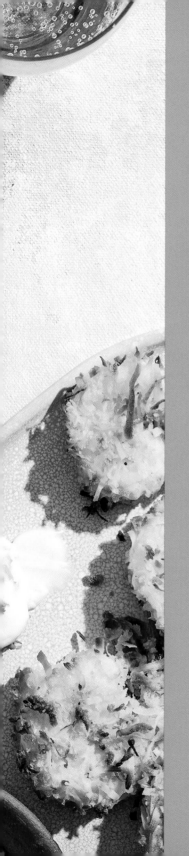

CHAPTER 6

FISH & SEAFOOD

COCONUT and PANKO SHRIMP

GLUTEN-FREE (use GF panko bread crumbs)

DAIRY-FREE

PREP TIME: 10 MINUTES

COOK TIME: 6 MINUTES

YIELD: 4 SERVINGS

1 pound jumbo shrimp, peeled and deveined, tails left on

½ cup all-purpose flour

¾ teaspoon kosher salt

¼ teaspoon garlic powder

¼ teaspoon ground black pepper

2 large eggs

¾ cup unsweetened shredded coconut

¾ cup panko bread crumbs

Avocado oil or other neutral-flavored oil, for spraying

⅓ cup chili garlic sauce (page 285)

¼ cup mayonnaise (page 276)

I had to make my own air-fried take on crispy shrimp after enjoying delicious versions at restaurants and food trucks all over Maui, Hawaii. The jumbo coconut shrimp at Da Nani Pirates food truck, in particular, were fantastic and inspired this version. Serve the shrimp as an appetizer with sweet chili sauce or "plate lunch"—style with rice alongside.

Pat the shrimp dry with paper towels.

Create a breading station with three shallow bowls: In the first bowl, stir together the flour, salt, garlic powder, and pepper until evenly mixed. In the second bowl, beat the eggs until no streaks remain. In the third bowl, stir together the coconut and bread crumbs until evenly mixed.

Grabbing the tail, dredge 1 shrimp in the flour, then shake any excess flour back into the bowl. Next, dip the shrimp in the eggs, holding it over the bowl for a few seconds to let any excess egg drip back into the bowl. Finally, place the shrimp in the bowl of bread crumbs and coconut and gently toss, making sure to coat all sides evenly. Transfer the breaded shrimp to the air frying basket. Repeat with the remaining shrimp until all are coated.

Place the black enamel cooking pan in the bottom oven rack position to catch any drips. Place the wire metal oven rack in the second highest position.

recipe continues

Preheat the oven on **AIR FRY** at 400°F and set the cooking time for 6 minutes.

Spray the shrimp lightly with the avocado oil.

Air fry the shrimp in the preheated oven. When the "**turn food**" message comes on, use tongs to flip the shrimp. Spray their second side with oil, then return them to the oven.

While the shrimp are cooking, make the dipping sauce: In a small bowl, stir together the chili garlic sauce and mayonnaise.

When the cooking program ends, transfer the shrimp to a serving platter or plates. Serve right away with the dipping sauce alongside.

Nutrition Information: Per serving (shrimp and sauce): 244 calories, 8 grams fat, 21 grams carbohydrates, 2 grams fiber, 19 grams protein

OLIVE OIL–POACHED SHRIMP with GARLIC and PARSLEY

GLUTEN-FREE, DAIRY-FREE

PREP TIME: 5 MINUTES, PLUS
30 MINUTES TO BRINE
COOK TIME: 9 MINUTES
YIELD: 4 SERVINGS

3 cups cold water

2 teaspoons kosher salt

12 ounces peeled and deveined
medium shrimp (41–50 per
pound)

4 cloves garlic, crushed or
minced

1 teaspoon chopped fresh
parsley

½ teaspoon red pepper flakes

¼ cup olive oil

½ baguette or other crusty
artisan bread, cut into
½-inch-thick slices, for
serving

To ensure that these shrimp are perfectly seasoned, firm, and juicy, they get a quick brine in salt water, then they are cooked in a generous amount of olive oil seasoned with garlic, parsley, and red pepper flakes. Serve them right out of the baking dish, with crusty bread for sopping up all of the flavorful oil. I love to serve this as a first course for four people, or as a whole meal for two, with a simple dinner salad alongside.

In a bowl, stir together the water and salt until the salt is fully dissolved. Add the shrimp. Cover and leave in the refrigerator to brine for 30 minutes.

Drain the shrimp in a colander, then pat them dry with paper towels.

Preheat the oven on **BAKE** at 350°F and set the cooking time for 9 minutes.

Place the shrimp in a 28-ounce Pyrex Littles baking dish or other small (1-quart) ceramic or glass baking dish. Add the garlic, parsley, red pepper flakes, and oil, and stir to combine.

Place the baking dish on top of the cooking pan. Bake the shrimp in the preheated oven. When the "**turn food**" message comes on, give the shrimp a stir, then return them to the oven.

When the cooking program ends, wearing heat-resistant mitts, remove the baking dish from the oven. Stir the shrimp once more. Serve the shrimp right away with the crusty bread alongside.

Nutrition Information: Per serving: 366 calories, 16 grams fat, 29 grams carbohydrates, 3 grams fiber, 22 grams protein

BACON-WRAPPED SCALLOPS

GLUTEN-FREE, DAIRY-FREE

PREP TIME: 5 MINUTES
COOK TIME: 10 MINUTES
YIELD: 3 SERVINGS

1 pound large sea scallops
(10 scallops or less)
10 slices bacon (the thinner
the better)
¼ teaspoon kosher salt
¼ teaspoon ground black
pepper
Olive oil, for spraying
Lemon wedges, for serving

Get the biggest, juiciest scallops you can find to make these bacon-wrapped beauties. Look for the U10 size, which means there are 10 or less scallops in a pound. They're pricey but worth it, and their large size means that they'll still be tender in the middle when the bacon is cooked through. Serve them as an appetizer or first course, over pasta (as pictured), or alongside steaks (page 137) for a luxurious surf and turf dinner.

Pat the scallops dry with paper towels. Wrap a piece of bacon around the outside of each scallop, then place them in the air frying basket.

Place the black enamel cooking pan in the bottom oven rack position. Place the wire metal oven rack in the second highest position.

Preheat the oven on **AIR FRY** at 400°F and set the cooking time for 10 minutes.

Season the scallops with the salt and pepper, then spray them lightly with oil.

Air fry the scallops in the preheated oven.

When the cooking program ends, use tongs to transfer the scallops to a serving platter or plates. Serve right away with lemon wedges alongside.

Nutrition Information: Per serving: 201 calories, 10 grams fat, 4 grams carbohydrates, 0 grams fiber, 24 grams protein

MISO-GLAZED SALMON

GLUTEN-FREE, DAIRY-FREE

PREP TIME: 5 MINUTES
COOK TIME: 18 MINUTES
YIELD: 4 SERVINGS

2 (8-ounce) skin-on salmon fillets (1½ to 2 inches thick in the middle)
Olive oil, for spraying
¼ teaspoon kosher salt
Pinch ground black pepper
Lemon wedges, for serving

MISO GLAZE

1 tablespoon white miso
2 tablespoons brown sugar
1 teaspoon rice vinegar
2 cloves garlic, crushed or grated on a Microplane
¼ teaspoon ground ginger or 1 teaspoon minced ginger root (from a ½-inch piece)
Pinch cayenne pepper

NOTE

If the salmon fillets are thinner than 1½ inches, you may need to lower the cooking time. This will usually be the case for smaller varieties of salmon. If this is the case, you'll still want to give the miso glaze ample time to bake. Spread it over thinner fillets after 5 minutes of cooking rather than waiting for the "**turn food**" message to come on, then bake until they reach 145°F in the thickest part of the fillet.

Baking is one of the more foolproof ways to prepare salmon—it always comes out beautifully tender. Here, it's topped with a savory-sweet miso glaze that bakes on during the last few minutes of cooking. For a light and nutritious dinner, serve this with quinoa or rice and a salad or slaw alongside.

Preheat the oven on **BAKE** at 350°F and set the cooking time for 18 minutes. Line the cooking pan with aluminum foil.

Place the salmon fillets skin side down on the lined cooking pan. Spray the fish lightly with oil and sprinkle with the salt and pepper. Bake the salmon in the preheated oven.

While the salmon is baking, make the miso glaze: In a small bowl, stir together the miso, brown sugar, vinegar, garlic, ginger, and cayenne.

When the "**turn food**" message comes on, wearing heat-resistant mitts, remove the cooking pan from the oven. Use a small spatula or spoon to spread the miso glaze over the fish. Return the salmon to the oven.

When the cooking program ends, use an instant-read thermometer to check the internal temperature of the salmon. It should be at least 145°F in the thickest part of the fillet. If it is not yet up to temperature, cook for a few more minutes.

Transfer the salmon to serving plates. Serve with lemon wedges.

Nutrition Information: Per serving: 228 calories, 12 grams fat, 7 grams carbohydrates, 0 grams fiber, 22 grams protein

CASHEW-CRUSTED MAHI MAHI

GLUTEN-FREE (use GF panko bread crumbs)
DAIRY-FREE

PREP TIME: 10 MINUTES
COOK TIME: 15 MINUTES
YIELD: 3 SERVINGS

3 (4-ounce) mahi mahi fillets
¼ teaspoon kosher salt
⅛ teaspoon ground black pepper
¼ cup all-purpose flour
½ teaspoon Old Bay seasoning
1 large egg
¾ cup raw cashews, finely chopped
¼ cup panko bread crumbs
Avocado oil or other neutral-flavored oil, for spraying

A Hawaii-inspired dish, this mahi mahi stays moist beneath a crunchy layer of chopped nuts. On the first evening of our baby-moon in Maui, my husband and I stopped in for dinner at the Tommy Bahama store in a shopping mall (Who knew they had restaurants? Not me!) and enjoyed a similar dish made with macadamia nuts. I've replaced macadamias with less expensive, easier to find, and equally delicious cashews. Serve the fillets with rice and asparagus (page 217) or another vegetable side dish.

Pat the fish dry with paper towels, then sprinkle it with the salt and pepper.

Create a breading station with three shallow bowls: In the first bowl, stir together the flour and Old Bay until evenly mixed. In the second bowl, whisk the egg until no streaks remain. In the third bowl, stir together the cashews and bread crumbs until evenly mixed.

Line the air frying basket with parchment paper and spray it lightly with oil.

Dredge 1 fish fillet in the flour, then shake any excess flour back into the bowl. Next, dip the fillet in the egg, holding it over the bowl for a few seconds to let any excess egg drip back into the bowl. Finally, place the fillet in the bowl of cashews and bread crumbs and gently toss, making sure to coat all sides evenly. Transfer the breaded fillet to the air frying basket. Repeat with the remaining fillets.

recipe continues

Place the black enamel cooking pan in the bottom oven rack position. Place the wire metal oven rack in the second highest position.

Preheat the oven on **AIR FRY** at 350°F and set the cooking time for 15 minutes.

Spray the fillets lightly with oil.

Air fry the fish in the preheated oven. When the "**turn food**" message comes on, use a thin flexible spatula to flip the fillets, then return them to the oven.

When the cooking program ends, transfer the fish fillets to serving plates and serve.

Nutrition Information: Per serving: 330 calories, 17 grams fat, 15 grams carbohydrates, 1 gram fiber, 30 grams protein

TORTILLA CHIP TILAPIA

GLUTEN-FREE (use GF flour blend)
DAIRY-FREE

PREP TIME: 10 MINUTES
COOK TIME: 12 MINUTES
YIELD: 4 SERVINGS

4 ounces corn tortilla chips
(about 4 dozen)

1 tablespoon chopped fresh
cilantro

1½ teaspoons chili powder

½ teaspoon ground cumin

½ teaspoon garlic powder

½ teaspoon kosher salt

⅓ cup all-purpose flour

1 large egg

1 tablespoon water

4 (4-ounce) tilapia fillets

Tartar sauce (page 277), salsa
verde (page 275), or salsa
ranchera (page 274), for
serving

Funnily enough, this recipe was inspired by the breaded tilapia fillets served in the cafeteria of a Silicon Valley tech company. My husband and I jokingly called it "Christmas fish," because the breading contained mysterious red and green flecks of unknown origin. Here, tortilla chips are combined with cilantro and spices to make the crunchy coating. Serve the fish with rice and beans, and tartar sauce (page 277) or salsa verde (page 275) on the side.

In a food processor, combine the tortilla chips, cilantro, chili powder, cumin, garlic powder, and salt. Pulse until the chips are finely crushed.

Create a breading station with three shallow bowls: Add the flour to the first bowl. In the second bowl, whisk the egg and water until no streaks remain. Add the crushed tortilla chip mixture to the third bowl.

Dredge a tilapia fillet in the flour, then shake any excess flour back into the bowl. Next, dip the fillet in the egg mixture, holding it over the bowl for a few seconds to let any excess egg drip back into the bowl. Finally, place the fillet in the bowl of tortilla chip crumbs, flipping it to coat both sides evenly and pressing down a bit so that the crumbs adhere well. Transfer the fillet to the air frying basket. Repeat with the remaining fillets.

Place the black enamel cooking pan in the bottom oven rack position. Place the wire metal oven rack in the second highest position.

recipe continues

FISH & SEAFOOD   **203**

NOTE

If the fillets are larger than 4 ounces, you may have to add a few minutes to the cooking time, and they may not all fit in the air frying basket at one time. If this is the case, air fry them in two batches.

Preheat the oven on **AIR FRY** at 375°F and set the cooking time for 12 minutes.

Air fry the fish in the preheated oven. When the "**turn food**" message comes on, use a thin flexible spatula to flip the fillets, then return them to the oven.

When the cooking program ends, use an instant-read thermometer to make sure the thickest part of each fillet has reached 145°F. Transfer the fillets to serving plates. Serve with tartar sauce or salsa on the side.

Nutrition Information: Per serving: 259 calories, 9 grams fat, 21 grams carbohydrates, 2 grams fiber, 25 grams protein

HOMEMADE FISH STICK TACOS

GLUTEN-FREE (use GF flour blend
and GF panko bread crumbs)
DAIRY-FREE

PREP TIME: 10 MINUTES
COOK TIME: 10 MINUTES
YIELD: 6 TACOS (3 SERVINGS)

1 pound cod or other white fish
    fillets
⅓ cup all-purpose flour
2 large eggs
2 tablespoons water
1 cup panko bread crumbs
1½ teaspoons Old Bay
    seasoning
Olive oil, for spraying
6 taco-size corn tortillas,
    warmed
½ cup tartar sauce (page 277)
1½ cups shredded red cabbage
Leaves only from 6 sprigs
    cilantro

Homemade fish sticks are tastier than the frozen kind, and you can choose any variety of fish you like to make them. I like to use panko bread crumbs to make them extra crispy, but regular bread crumbs are good, too. Serve as fish tacos, topped with homemade tartar sauce, shredded cabbage, and cilantro, or straight up as a kid-friendly main dish, with rice and veggies alongside.

Pat the fish fillets dry with paper towels, then cut them into 1-inch-thick strips.

Create a breading station with three shallow bowls: Add the flour to the first bowl. In the second bowl, whisk the eggs and water until no streaks remain. In the third bowl, stir together the bread crumbs and Old Bay seasoning until evenly mixed.

Line the air frying basket with parchment paper. Place the black enamel cooking pan in the bottom oven rack position to catch any drips. Place the wire metal oven rack in the second highest position.

Dredge a strip of fish in the flour, then shake any excess flour back into the bowl. Next, dip the fish in the eggs, holding it over the bowl for a few seconds to let any excess egg drip back into the bowl. Finally, place the fish in the bowl of bread crumbs, flipping it to coat both sides evenly and pressing down a bit so that the crumbs adhere well. Transfer the fish to the lined air frying basket. Repeat with the remaining strips.

recipe continues

Preheat the oven on **AIR FRY** at 375°F and set the cooking time for 10 minutes.

Spray the fish sticks lightly with the oil.

Air fry the fish sticks in the preheated oven. When the "**turn food**" message comes on, use a thin flexible spatula to flip the fish sticks. Spray them lightly with oil, then return them to the oven.

When the cooking program ends, wearing heat-resistant mitts, remove the fish sticks from the oven. Assemble the fish tacos: Place the warmed tortillas on serving plates, then top them with the fish sticks, tartar sauce, cabbage, and cilantro. Serve right away.

Nutrition Information: Per serving (2 tacos): 410 calories, 25 grams fat, 30 grams carbohydrates, 4 grams fiber, 19 grams protein

LEMON BUTTER COD FILLETS

GLUTEN-FREE

PREP TIME: 5 MINUTES
COOK TIME: 13 MINUTES
YIELD: 4 SERVINGS

4 (6-ounce) Pacific cod fillet portions (¾ inch thick)

2 tablespoons unsalted butter, melted and cooled

1 tablespoon fresh lemon juice

¼ teaspoon kosher salt

⅛ teaspoon ground black pepper

2 teaspoons chopped fresh parsley

Tartar sauce (page 277), for serving

NOTE

This recipe also works well with other varieties of white fish, such as haddock, pollock, or halibut. You may need to adjust the cooking time based on the thickness of the fish. For all varieties, use an instant-read thermometer to check for an internal temperature of at least 145°F.

Cod fillets have a mild, crowd-pleasing flavor, and they stand up well to high-heat cooking. This is a very simple preparation and the way I prepare them most often—the fillets are simply baked in melted butter and tangy lemon juice. I like to serve them with tartar sauce (page 277), roasted vegetables (page 216), and rice for a meal pulled straight from my childhood memories of seafood dinners on the California coast.

Preheat the oven on **BAKE** at 375°F and set the cooking time for 13 minutes. Line the cooking pan with aluminum foil or parchment paper.

Place the cod fillets on the lined cooking pan. Pour the butter and lemon juice over the fish, then sprinkle the fish with the salt and pepper.

Bake the fish in the preheated oven.

When the cooking program ends, use an instant-read thermometer to check the internal temperature of the fish. It should be at least 145°F in the thickest part of each fillet. If it has not yet come up to temperature, bake for a couple more minutes and test again.

Transfer the fish to serving plates and sprinkle the parsley on top. Serve right away with tartar sauce on the side.

Nutrition Information: Per serving: 205 calories, 13 grams fat, 2 grams carbohydrates, 0 grams fiber, 30 grams protein

CHAPTER 7

VEGETABLE SIDES

CRISPY BRUSSELS SPROUTS and GARLIC CLOVES

VEGAN, GLUTEN-FREE

PREP TIME: 5 MINUTES
COOK TIME: 18 MINUTES
YIELD: 6 SERVINGS

1½ pounds Brussels sprouts, halved lengthwise or quartered if very large

24 cloves garlic, peeled (from 2 bulbs, or store-bought already peeled)

1 tablespoon olive oil

½ teaspoon kosher salt

¼ teaspoon ground black pepper

NOTE
If you like, you can add chopped fresh parsley and grated parmesan cheese after cooking. Alternatively, the sprouts are delicious served with shawarma sauce (page 278) spooned over them.

When I was little, my mom would always steam Brussels sprouts, and I liked them well enough, but they weren't something I craved. Now I prefer to air fry them until they're deeply browned and crispy on the outside, which is a huge improvement. A generous handful of whole garlic cloves get caramelized and browned along with the sprouts, and together they make for an irresistible side dish.

Place the black enamel cooking pan in the bottom oven rack position to catch any drips. Place the wire metal oven rack in the second highest position.

Preheat the oven on **AIR FRY** at 375°F and set the cooking time for 18 minutes.

In a large mixing bowl, toss the Brussels sprouts and garlic cloves with the olive oil, salt, and pepper. Pour the sprouts and garlic into the air frying basket and spread them out in an even layer.

Air fry the sprouts in the preheated oven. When the "**turn food**" message comes on, stir the Brussels sprouts and garlic, then return them to the oven.

When the cooking program ends, transfer the sprouts and garlic to a serving bowl and serve right away.

Nutrition Information: Per serving: 70 calories, 2 grams fat, 11 grams carbohydrates, 3 grams fiber, 3 grams protein

BROCCOLI and CAULIFLOWER with CHEESE SAUCE

GLUTEN-FREE (use GF flour blend)

PREP TIME: 5 MINUTES
COOK TIME: 10 MINUTES
YIELD: 6 SERVINGS

1 pound broccoli florets
 (2 large crowns)
1 pound cauliflower florets
 (1 small cauliflower)
1 tablespoon olive oil
¼ teaspoon kosher salt
⅛ teaspoon ground black
 pepper

CHEESE SAUCE
2 tablespoons unsalted butter
2 tablespoons all-purpose
 flour
1 cup half-and-half
1½ cups grated sharp cheddar
 cheese
¼ teaspoon kosher salt
¼ teaspoon garlic powder
¼ teaspoon mustard powder
⅛ teaspoon cayenne pepper

It's extra fun to eat your veggies when they're covered in a creamy and thick cheddar cheese sauce. Broccoli and cauliflower take 10 minutes to cook to tender-crisp perfection in the air fryer oven, while you whip up the quick cheese sauce on the stove or in an Instant Pot. Look on page 216 for a mac 'n cheese variation.

Preheat the oven on **BAKE** at 350°F and set the cooking time for 10 minutes for al dente vegetables or 15 minutes for more well-done, browner vegetables (the broccoli florets will be quite crispy). Line the cooking pan with parchment paper or aluminum foil.

Combine the broccoli and cauliflower in a large mixing bowl. Drizzle with the oil and sprinkle with salt and pepper, then toss well to coat the vegetables. Spread out the vegetables on the lined cooking pan.

Bake the vegetables in the preheated oven.

While the vegetables are baking, make the sauce on the stovetop or in an Instant Pot: In a saucepan over medium heat, or in an Instant Pot on its **SAUTE** program, melt the butter. Add the flour and cook for 1 minute, whisking constantly, until the roux is bubbling but not browned. In a thin stream, pour in the half-and-half, continuing to whisk constantly to prevent lumps.

recipe continues

Let the sauce come up to a simmer. Turn the heat down to low and simmer for 2 to 3 minutes, just until the sauce is beginning to thicken. Remove the pot from the heat. Whisk in the grated cheese, salt, garlic powder, mustard powder, and cayenne, whisking until the cheese is completely melted and the sauce is smooth.

Transfer the vegetables to a serving bowl or plates. Pour the cheese sauce over the vegetables and serve.

Nutrition Information: Per serving: 258 calories, 19 grams fat, 11 grams carbohydrates, 3 grams fiber, 12 grams protein

VARIATION · VEGGIE MAC 'N CHEESE Double the cheese sauce. Cook 1 pound pasta such as elbows or rotini according to package directions. Drain the pasta and stir it into the sauce along with the vegetables.

BASIC ROASTED VEGETABLES

You can use this recipe as a basic template for roasting up to 2 pounds of other vegetables. I often do a mix of carrots, zucchini, cauliflower, green beans, and broccoli. Slice zucchini and carrots into ¼-inch-thick coins, and cut the cauliflower, green beans, and broccoli into bite-size pieces. Toss the vegetables with oil (1½ teaspoons per pound of vegetables) and any seasonings you like, and **BAKE** at 350°F for 10 minutes for al dente vegetables or 15 minutes for well-done vegetables. Cut harder vegetables such as winter squash into 1-inch pieces, toss with oil and seasonings, and **BAKE** at 350°F for 20 minutes.

HERBED ASPARAGUS and LEMON

VEGAN, GLUTEN-FREE

PREP TIME: 5 MINUTES
COOK TIME: 4 MINUTES
YIELD: 4 SERVINGS

1 pound asparagus spears

½ lemon, seeded and quartered

Olive oil, for spraying

¼ teaspoon Italian seasoning

¼ teaspoon kosher salt

⅛ teaspoon garlic powder

⅛ teaspoon ground black pepper

A super simple side dish for springtime, when in-season asparagus is plump and tender and needs very little to make it delicious. Wedges of lemon get extra juicy when they're air fried right along with the asparagus. You can make this recipe with thin or thick spears of asparagus—the cooking time will vary by a few minutes.

Trim or snap off the last 2 inches or so of each spear of asparagus, where it begins to become woody and fibrous.

Place the black enamel cooking pan in the bottom oven rack position to catch any drips. Place the wire metal oven rack in the second highest position.

Preheat the oven on **AIR FRY** at 400°F and set the cooking time for 4 minutes for thin asparagus spears, 6 minutes for medium, or 8 minutes for thick.

Arrange the asparagus spears in a single layer in the air frying basket, then place the lemon pieces in the basket around the asparagus, cut side up. Spray the asparagus and lemon lightly with the oil, then sprinkle the Italian seasoning, salt, garlic powder, and pepper evenly over the asparagus.

Air fry the asparagus in the preheated oven.

When the cooking program ends, use tongs to transfer the asparagus and lemon to a serving dish. Squeeze the lemon over the asparagus and serve.

Nutrition Information: Per serving: 38 calories, 1 gram fat, 6 grams carbohydrates, 2 grams fiber, 3 grams protein

BLACK BEAN GARLIC GREEN BEANS

VEGAN

PREP TIME: 5 MINUTES
COOK TIME: 12 MINUTES
YIELD: 4 TO 6 SERVINGS

1 pound green beans, stem ends trimmed

1 tablespoon Chinese black bean garlic sauce (Lee Kum Kee brand)

1½ teaspoons olive oil

Sesame seeds, for garnish (optional)

Black bean garlic sauce is one of my favorite condiments to have on hand. It packs so much savory, salty flavor that one tablespoon will season an entire pound of green beans! I will often make a weeknight dinner out of these with some rice cooked in the Instant Pot and Sesame-Soy Tofu (page 124).

Place the black enamel cooking pan in the bottom oven rack position to catch any drips. Place the wire metal oven rack in the second highest position.

Preheat the oven on **AIR FRY** at 400°F and set the cooking time for 12 minutes.

In a large mixing bowl, toss together the green beans, black bean sauce, and oil until the green beans are evenly coated. Spread out the green beans in the air frying basket in an even layer.

Air fry the green beans in the preheated oven.

When the cooking program ends, use tongs to transfer the green beans to a serving bowl or plates. Serve right away.

Nutrition Information: Per serving: 81 calories, 5 grams fat, 8 grams carbohydrates, 3 grams fiber, 2 grams protein

VARIATION · BASIC GREEN BEANS Omit the black bean garlic sauce. Toss the green beans with 1½ teaspoons olive oil, ½ teaspoon garlic salt, and a pinch ground black pepper. Air fry as in the main recipe.

ZUCCHINI and CARROTS with PEA PISTOU

VEGAN, GLUTEN-FREE

PREP TIME: 10 MINUTES
COOK TIME: 15 MINUTES
YIELD: 6 SERVINGS

1 pound zucchini, trimmed

1 pound carrots, peeled

1 tablespoon olive oil

¼ teaspoon kosher salt

⅛ teaspoon ground black pepper

PEA PISTOU

1 clove garlic, peeled

1 cup loosely packed fresh flat-leaf parsley leaves

½ cup frozen peas, thawed

½ teaspoon grated lemon zest

¼ cup olive oil

¼ teaspoon kosher salt, plus more if you like

VARIATION   CHEESY PISTOU

Omit the lemon zest. Add ¼ cup grated parmesan, pecorino, or Cotija cheese.

In this side dish for spring and summer, roasted vegetables are topped with pistou, a sauce similar to pesto. My vegan version includes some peas, so you get some natural sweetness plus even more veggies in every bite. I use a crinkle cutter to make the zucchini and carrots easier to grab so my toddler eats them as finger food, while we enjoy them as a side dish alongside roast chicken (page 166) or tri-tip roast (page 134).

Use a crinkle cutter or chef's knife to cut the zucchini and carrots into ¼-inch-thick rounds.

Preheat the oven on **ROAST** at 350°F and set the cooking time for 15 minutes. Line the cooking pan with parchment or foil.

In a large mixing bowl, toss together the zucchini, carrots, oil, salt, and pepper. Spread the vegetables on the cooking pan in an even layer. Roast the zucchini and carrots in the preheated oven.

While the vegetables are roasting, make the pistou: On a cutting board, chop the garlic, parsley, and peas all together for a few minutes, until you have a finely chopped mixture. Transfer the mixture to a bowl. Add the lemon zest, oil, and salt and stir to combine. Taste for seasoning and add more salt, if you like.

When the cooking program ends, transfer the zucchini and carrots to a serving bowl or plates. Spoon the pistou over the vegetables and serve right away.

Nutrition Information: Per serving: 228 calories, 18 grams fat, 17 grams carbohydrates, 5 grams fiber, 3 grams protein

BLISTERED CARROTS and RADISHES

VEGAN, GLUTEN-FREE

PREP TIME: 5 MINUTES
COOK TIME: 15 MINUTES
YIELD: 4 SERVINGS

1 pound carrots (6 medium), peeled

1 bunch radishes, trimmed

2 teaspoons olive oil

1 clove garlic, pressed or minced

½ teaspoon chopped fresh rosemary

¼ teaspoon kosher salt

⅛ teaspoon ground black pepper

VARIATION This method also works nicely for butternut or other winter squash, cut into ¾-inch cubes. Substitute 1½ pounds squash, peeled, seeded, and cubed, for the carrots and radishes. Everything else remains the same.

My parents never cooked radishes when I was a kid—we only had them raw in salads or with dip. Roasted radishes are a revelation—cooking tames their spicy flavor, and the high heat of the air fryer oven gives them a beautiful, blistered appearance while still being juicy on the inside. The sweeter carrots complement radishes well, for an easy and fast weeknight side dish.

Roll-cut the carrots into ¾-inch-long pieces. For a rustic appearance, cut them on the bias, rotating the carrot a half-turn after each slice. Halve the radishes, or quarter them if they are very large.

Place the black enamel cooking pan in the bottom oven rack position to catch any drips. Place the wire metal oven rack in the second highest position.

Preheat the oven on **AIR FRY** at 400°F and set the cooking time for 15 minutes.

In a large mixing bowl, toss the carrots and radishes with the oil, garlic, rosemary, salt, and pepper until the vegetables are evenly coated. Spread out the vegetables in the air frying basket in a single layer.

Air fry the vegetables in the preheated oven.

When the cooking program ends, transfer the vegetables to a serving bowl or plates and serve.

Nutrition Information: Per serving: 73 calories, 3 grams fat, 12 grams carbohydrates, 4 grams fiber, 1 gram protein

CABBAGE WEDGES
with SOY SAUCE and BUTTER

VEGAN (substitute vegan butter for the butter)
GLUTEN-FREE (substitute GF tamari for the soy sauce)

PREP TIME: 5 MINUTES
COOK TIME: 12 MINUTES
YIELD: 4 SERVINGS

½ medium head green cabbage
2 tablespoons unsalted butter, melted
1 tablespoon soy sauce

VARIATION You can also make this recipe with 1 pound coarsely chopped cabbage rather than cutting it into wedges. When the "**turn food**" message comes on, drizzle the soy sauce over and stir until well mixed.

All of the ingredients in this recipe are in the name. The surprising and simple combination makes for a savory side dish that comes together quickly. You'll use half a head of cabbage for this recipe—either ask the produce manager at the grocery store to sell you a half-head, or buy a whole cabbage and save the rest to make coleslaw (page 157) on another day.

Line the cooking pan with aluminum foil or parchment paper.

Lay the cabbage cut side down on a cutting board. Slice it into 8 (1½-inch-thick) wedges, leaving the core end of each wedge intact. Lay the wedges flat on the lined cooking pan.

Preheat the oven on **ROAST** at 375°F and set the cooking time for 12 minutes.

Drizzle the butter over the cabbage wedges.

Roast the cabbage in the preheated oven. When the "**turn food**" message comes on, use tongs to flip the cabbage. Drizzle the soy sauce over the cabbage, then return it to the oven.

When the cooking program ends, transfer the wedges to serving plates and serve.

Nutrition Information: Per serving: 77 calories, 6 grams fat, 6 grams carbohydrates, 3 grams fiber, 2 grams protein

TAPAS-STYLE PEPPERS

VEGAN, GLUTEN-FREE

PREP TIME: 5 MINUTES
COOK TIME: 5 MINUTES
YIELD: 4 SERVINGS AS AN
APPETIZER

10 ounces Padron or shishito
    peppers (about 2 dozen),
    left whole, or 1 dozen mini
    sweet peppers, halved
    lengthwise and seeded
1 teaspoon olive oil
⅛ teaspoon kosher salt

When Spanish Padron peppers are in season from May through September, I scoop them up at the farmers' market whenever I can. The early-season peppers tend to be milder, but regardless of harvest time, about one in ten will be much spicier than the others! They're best enjoyed in a simple preparation with a drizzle of olive oil and a sprinkle of salt. If you can't find Padron peppers, shishitos or even mini sweet peppers are good this way, too.

Place the black enamel cooking pan in the bottom oven rack position to catch any drips. Place the wire metal oven rack in the second highest position.

Preheat the oven on **AIR FRY** at 400°F and set the cooking time for 5 minutes.

In a large mixing bowl, toss the peppers with the oil and salt until evenly coated. Spread them out in a single layer in the air frying basket.

Air fry the peppers in the preheated oven.

When the cooking program ends, transfer the peppers to a serving platter or bowl and serve.

Nutrition Information: Per serving: 43 calories, 1 gram fat, 7 grams carbohydrates, 2 grams fiber, 1 gram protein

MAPLE and BUTTER ACORN SQUASH

VEGAN (substitute vegan butter for the butter)
GLUTEN-FREE

PREP TIME: 5 MINUTES
COOK TIME: 22 MINUTES
YIELD: 4 SERVINGS

2 small acorn squashes
  (1½ pounds each)
4 tablespoons unsalted butter,
  melted and cooled
⅓ cup maple syrup
½ teaspoon ground cinnamon
¼ teaspoon ground nutmeg
½ teaspoon kosher salt

When I was growing up, my mom made acorn squash for us this way every fall, except of course she baked them in a traditional oven, so they took more than twice as long to cook. This sped-up air fryer oven version is just as wonderful. Each squash half acts as a vessel for a rich and sweet combination of butter, maple syrup, and spices. Serve the squash as a vegetable side dish—or even with a scoop of vanilla ice cream in the middle for dessert.

Line the cooking pan with aluminum foil or parchment paper.

Place the squashes on a cutting board and cut them in half from stem to tip. Use a spoon to scoop out and discard the seeds and stringy flesh. Place the scooped-out squash halves cut side up on the cutting board—if they do not sit perfectly level, trim off a small piece on the bottom to make them do so. Transfer the halves to the cooking pan.

Preheat the oven on **BAKE** at 375°F and set the cooking time for 22 minutes.

Use a pastry brush to brush the butter on the cut edges of the squashes, then pour the remaining butter into the squash cavities. Pour the maple syrup into the squash cavities. Sprinkle in the cinnamon, nutmeg, and salt.

Bake the squashes in the preheated oven.

When the cooking program ends, check the squashes for doneness —you should be able to pierce the flesh easily with a fork. If they are not cooked through, bake for a few more minutes.

Carefully transfer the squashes to serving plates and serve.

Nutrition Information: Per serving: 216 calories, 11 grams fat, 30 grams carbohydrates, 2 grams fiber, 1 gram protein

POTATO LATKES

DAIRY-FREE (use vegan sour cream)

PREP TIME: 25 MINUTES
COOK TIME: 18 MINUTES
YIELD: 12 LATKES (4 SERVINGS)

1½ pounds russet potatoes
  (3 medium)
¾ teaspoon kosher salt
1 medium yellow onion
1 large egg, beaten
⅓ cup plain bread crumbs
  (page 296) or matzo meal
Avocado oil or other neutral-
  flavored oil, for spraying

As a Jewish woman who looks forward to latkes for Hanukkah every year, I had to take on the holy grail: the air fryer latke. While no air-fried version is going to be as rich and indulgent as latkes cooked in a pan full of oil, these really are delicious, and as a bonus, my house doesn't smell like frying oil and onions for days after I make them! Serve latkes with the traditional applesauce and sour cream or as an appetizer topped with cream cheese, smoked salmon, capers, and chopped red onions.

Peel the potatoes and cut them into quarters lengthwise. Grate them on a coarse grater into a large mixing bowl. Toss the grated potatoes with ½ teaspoon of the salt. Let sit for 10 minutes.

Place the potatoes in the middle of a kitchen towel, gather up the sides, and wring them out over the sink as best you can, squeezing out as much water as possible. (Alternatively, you can use a nut milk bag, if you have one.)

Grate the onion onto a cutting board. Wipe out the mixing bowl, then add back the wrung-out potatoes. Add the remaining ¼ teaspoon salt, the egg, and bread crumbs to the potatoes. Add the onion, avoiding adding any liquid that has seeped out of them onto the cutting board. Stir the mixture until evenly combined.

Line the cooking pan with parchment paper.

Preheat the oven on **BAKE** at 375°F and set the cooking time for 18 minutes.

recipe continues

Use a ¼-cup measure to portion 12 scoops of the latke mixture on the lined cooking pan. Without compressing the mixture, use your fingers to shape each scoop into a circular patty, 3 inches in diameter. Spray the tops of the latkes liberally with oil.

Bake the latkes in the preheated oven. When the "**turn food**" message comes on, use a thin flexible spatula to flip the latkes. Spray them with oil on their second side, then return them to the oven.

When the cooking program ends, transfer the latkes to serving plates. Serve right away.

Nutrition Information: Per serving (3 latkes only): 205 calories, 5 grams fat, 36 grams carbohydrates, 3 grams fiber, 6 grams protein

PEPPERS and ONIONS

VEGAN, GLUTEN-FREE

PREP TIME: 5 MINUTES
COOK TIME: 10 MINUTES
YIELD: 4 SERVINGS

2 large bell peppers (red, yellow, orange, or a mix), seeded and cut into ¼-inch-thick strips

1 large yellow onion, cut into ¼-inch-thick slices

2 cloves garlic, crushed or minced

1 tablespoon olive oil

½ teaspoon dried oregano

¼ teaspoon kosher salt

Pinch cayenne (optional)

Roasted peppers and onions are a versatile side dish or meal component. Serve them alongside a main dish, spoon them onto a toasted hoagie or submarine roll with meatballs (page 147) or Italian sausage, chop them up and use them as a filling in egg bites (page 56) or breakfast burritos (page 59), or pile them into fajitas with slices of steak (page 134).

Preheat the oven on **ROAST** at 400°F and set the cooking time for 10 minutes. Line the cooking pan with parchment paper or aluminum foil.

In a large mixing bowl, combine the peppers, onion, garlic, oil, oregano, salt, and cayenne (if using). Toss to coat the peppers and onions evenly with the oil and seasonings. Spread out the peppers and onions in an even layer on the lined cooking pan.

Roast the peppers and onions in the preheated oven.

When the cooking program ends, transfer the peppers and onions to a serving bowl or plates and serve right away, or use however you like.

Nutrition Information: Per serving: 75 calories, 4 grams fat, 10 grams carbohydrates, 3 grams fiber, 2 grams protein

ONION RINGS

VEGAN (substitute unsweetened plant-based milk for the buttermilk)

GLUTEN-FREE (use GF flour blend and GF bread crumbs)

PREP TIME: 10 MINUTES

COOK TIME: 16 MINUTES

YIELD: 4 SERVINGS

1 large sweet yellow onion

¼ cup all-purpose flour

1 cup buttermilk or milk

½ cup all-purpose flour

1½ teaspoons seasoned salt (page 291)

1½ cups panko or plain bread crumbs

Avocado oil or other neutral-flavored oil, for spraying

Burger sauce (page 283) or ketchup (page 279), for serving

Onion rings are one of my favorite sides to make in the air fryer, since they are so fast to make and so much less greasy than the deep-fried kind. Use buttermilk for a thicker, more classic batter or regular milk for a thinner, shatteringly crisp result. The rings cook best in two batches so they don't stick together, but the cooking time is fast, just 8 minutes per batch. Enjoy them while they're still hot and crispy, dipped in burger sauce (page 283) or ketchup (page 279).

Line the air frying basket with parchment paper. Place the black enamel cooking pan in the bottom oven rack position to catch any drips. Place the wire metal oven rack in the second highest position.

Cut the onion into ½-inch slices, then separate the slices into individual rings. Place the rings in a large mixing bowl. Sprinkle the flour over the onion and toss with your hands until the rings are all evenly coated.

In a blender, combine the buttermilk, flour, and seasoned salt. Blend for about 20 seconds at medium speed, until smooth, scraping down the sides halfway through blending if needed.

Create a breading station with two shallow bowls: Pour the batter into the first bowl. Add the bread crumbs to the second bowl.

Dredge an onion ring in the batter, holding it over the bowl for a few seconds to let any excess batter drip back into the bowl. Next, place the onion ring in the bread crumbs, tossing it to coat evenly. Transfer the onion ring to the lined air frying basket and repeat until you have filled up the basket with a single layer. Do not stack the onion rings on top of each other, as they may stick together—it is best to air fry them in two batches.

Preheat the oven on **AIR FRY** at 400°F and set the cooking time for 8 minutes.

Spray the onion rings lightly with oil.

Air fry the onion rings in the preheated oven. When the "**turn food**" message comes on, use a thin flexible spatula to flip the onion rings. Spray their second side lightly with oil, then return them to the oven.

When the cooking program ends, transfer the onion rings to a serving platter and enjoy right away, or hold until the second batch is done. Repeat the breading and cooking steps for the remainder of the onion rings.

(If you are holding back the first batch to serve all of the onion rings together, when the second batch is done, add the first batch back to the air frying basket on top of second batch, then place them back in the oven for a couple minutes on its "**keep warm**" setting.)

Serve right away with burger sauce or ketchup on the side.

Nutrition Information: Per serving (onion rings only): 140 calories, 2 grams fat, 27 grams carbohydrates, 2 grams fiber, 4 grams protein

TATER TOTS with VEGAN MAYO and SPICY KETCHUP

VEGAN, GLUTEN-FREE

PREP TIME: 5 MINUTES
COOK TIME: 10 MINUTES
YIELD: 4 SERVINGS

1 pound frozen Tater Tots
¼ cup ketchup (page 279)
2 teaspoons sriracha sauce
¼ cup Lemony Vegan Mayonnaise (page 276)
1 green onion, sliced thinly

One of my favorite food destinations is Outside Lands, a music festival held every summer in San Francisco's Golden Gate Park. One vendor, The Japanese Pantry, serves up plates piled high with crisp Tater Tots drizzled with creamy mayo and spicy ketchup, with green onions sprinkled on top. In my version, the Tater Tots are still store-bought, but the homemade mayo (page 276) is vegan, so just about anyone can indulge in this festival treat.

Place the black enamel cooking pan in the bottom oven rack position to catch any drips. Place the wire metal oven rack in the second highest position.

Preheat the oven on **AIR FRY** at 400°F and set the cooking time for 10 minutes.

Spread out the Tater Tots in the air frying basket in a single layer.

Air fry the Tater Tots in the preheated oven. When the "**turn food**" message comes on, shake the basket gently to flip the tots, then return them to the oven.

While the tots are cooking, stir together the ketchup and sriracha sauce.

Transfer the Tater Tots to a serving platter or plates. Drizzle them with the spicy ketchup and mayo, then sprinkle the green onion on top. (Alternatively, you can serve the condiments on the side.) Serve right away.

Nutrition Information: Per serving: 238 calories, 14 grams fat, 26 grams carbohydrates, 2 grams fiber, 4 grams protein

STEAKHOUSE BAKED POTATOES

VEGAN (use vegan butter, vegan sour cream, vegan cheese shreds, and vegan bacon bits)

GLUTEN-FREE

PREP TIME: 5 MINUTES

COOK TIME: 45 MINUTES

YIELD: 4 SERVINGS

4 medium-large russet potatoes (8 ounces each)

2 teaspoons olive oil

½ teaspoon kosher salt

¼ teaspoon ground black pepper

TOPPINGS

4 tablespoons unsalted butter, cut into 4 pats

½ cup sour cream

1 cup shredded cheddar cheese

2 green onions, sliced

2 slices cooked bacon (page 64), crumbled

NOTE

If you are able to weigh the potatoes, that will help you judge the cooking time for smaller or larger ones than indicated in the recipe. My rule of thumb is as follows: 4-ounce russet potatoes take 25 minutes to cook through on **BAKE** at 400°F. For every additional ounce of weight per potato, add another 5 minutes to the cooking time.

These baked potatoes are done much faster than in a traditional oven, thanks to the air fryer oven's short preheating time and incredibly efficient heat. Topped with all of the traditional steakhouse fixings, they are a classic, crowd-pleasing side dish. If you're serving them with steak (page 137), bake the potatoes first, then keep them warm in a covered dish while the steaks are cooking. I find that one big potato with all the fixings is plenty for a meal all on its own. For a vegetarian meal or hearty side dish, top the potatoes with Broccoli and Cauliflower with Cheese Sauce (page 214) instead of the toppings listed below.

Preheat the oven on **BAKE** at 400°F and set the cooking time for 45 minutes. Line the cooking pan with aluminum foil.

In a large mixing bowl, drizzle the oil over the potatoes, then sprinkle on the salt and pepper. Use your hands to rub the oil and seasonings all over the potatoes, coating them evenly. Place the potatoes on the lined cooking pan.

Bake the potatoes in the preheated oven.

When the cooking program ends, wearing heat-resistant mitts, transfer the potatoes to serving plates. Make lengthwise and crosswise cuts in the potatoes, then use your hands to push in and up on the ends of the potatoes to split them open. Top each potato with a pat of butter, a dollop of sour cream, and sprinkles of cheddar cheese, green onions, and bacon. Serve right away.

Nutrition Information: Per serving: 502 calories, 32 grams fat, 42 grams carbohydrates, 4 grams fiber, 14 grams protein

ROASTED YUKON GOLD POTATOES

VEGAN, GLUTEN-FREE

PREP TIME: 5 MINUTES
COOK TIME: 18 MINUTES
YIELD: 4 SERVINGS

1½ pounds Yukon gold potatoes, cut into 1-inch cubes

1 tablespoon olive oil

½ teaspoon garlic powder

½ teaspoon sweet paprika

¼ teaspoon ground black pepper

½ teaspoon kosher salt

The texture of Yukon gold potatoes strikes the perfect balance between creamy and starchy. Because of this, they are my favorite potato to enjoy simply roasted, coated with a generous amount of seasonings and a touch of oil. Serve them with roasted chicken (page 166) or tri-tip roast (page 134), roasting them while the meat rests before carving.

Preheat the oven on **ROAST** at 390°F and set the cooking time for 18 minutes. Line the cooking pan with parchment paper or aluminum foil.

In a large mixing bowl, toss the potatoes with the olive oil, garlic powder, paprika, pepper, and salt. Spread the potatoes out in an even layer on the cooking pan.

Roast the potatoes in the preheated oven. When the "**turn food**" message comes on, use a spatula to flip the potatoes, then return them to the oven.

When the cooking program ends, transfer the potatoes to a serving bowl or plates and serve.

Nutrition Information: Per serving: 162 calories, 3 grams fat, 30 grams carbohydrates, 4 grams fiber, 4 grams protein

OLIVE OIL FRENCH FRIES

VEGAN, GLUTEN-FREE

PREP TIME: 10 MINUTES, PLUS
15 MINUTES TO SOAK
COOK TIME: 20 MINUTES
YIELD: 4 SERVINGS

1½ pounds russet potatoes
    (3 medium potatoes)
2 tablespoons olive oil
½ teaspoon kosher salt

Air fryers were pretty much made for french fries, and with the larger basket in an air fryer oven, you can make even more of them at a time. I use olive oil because I like the flavor, but feel free to use avocado oil or another neutral-flavored oil, if you like. To get extra crispy results, make sure to soak the cut potatoes in cold water, then give them a second toss in oil, as written below.

In a large mixing bowl, make an ice water bath with 1 quart cold water and 2 cups ice.

Peel the potatoes or leave them unpeeled, if you like. Use a chef's knife or a mandoline (with a cut-resistant glove on your cutting hand) to slice the potatoes into ¼-inch-thick batons (¼ inch might be thinner than you think; check a ruler if you're not sure). Place the potatoes in the ice water bath and let them soak for 15 minutes.

Lay out a large kitchen towel or a few paper towels on your work surface. Drain the potatoes in a colander and rinse with cold water. Spread them out on the towel in a single layer and pat them dry.

Dry the bowl, then return the potatoes to it. Drizzle 1 tablespoon of the olive oil over the potatoes, then toss well, until the potatoes are evenly coated.

Place the black enamel cooking pan in the bottom oven rack position to catch any drips. Place the wire metal oven rack in the second highest position.

recipe continues

NOTE

In the manuals for their air fryers, Instant Brands recommends
soaking the potatoes in cold
water before you air fry them.
This removes the coating of
starch from the outside of the
cut potatoes and keeps them
from overbrowning and sticking
together as they cook.

Preheat the oven on **AIR FRY** at 400°F and set the cooking time for 20 minutes for light golden fries or 23 minutes for well-done fries.

Transfer the potatoes to the air frying basket and spread them out in as even a layer as possible.

Air fry the potatoes in the preheated oven. When the "**turn food**" message comes on, return the fries to the bowl and gently toss them with the remaining 1 tablespoon olive oil. Spread them out again in the basket and return them to the oven.

When the cooking program ends, transfer the fries to serving plates. Sprinkle them with the salt while they are still hot, and serve right away.

Nutrition Information: Per serving: 184 calories, 7 grams fat, 28 grams carbohydrates, 2 grams fiber, 3 grams protein

VARIATIONS **TRUFFLE FRIES** Season the fries with ¼ teaspoon truffle salt and ¼ teaspoon kosher salt instead of all kosher salt, and garnish with 1 tablespoon chopped fresh parsley.
STEAKHOUSE FRIES Instead of skinny batons, cut the potatoes into 16 wedges each. Follow the rest of the recipe as written above, ex-cept adjust the cooking temperature and time to 375°F for 30 minutes.

CAJUN-SPICED SWEET POTATO FRIES

VEGAN, GLUTEN-FREE

PREP TIME: 5 MINUTES
COOK TIME: 13 MINUTES
YIELD: 4 SERVINGS

1½ pounds sweet potatoes
   (2 large)
2 teaspoons olive oil
1 teaspoon Cajun spice blend
¼ teaspoon salt
Ketchup (page 279) or
   Sriracha Mayo (page 276),
   for serving

Cajun spices go so well with sweet potatoes—I love the combination of hot and sweet. These fries are great dipped in ketchup (page 279) or mayonnaise. Look to the recipe for Lemony Vegan Mayonnaise (page 276) for a sriracha-spiked variation if you're craving even more spice.

Peel the sweet potatoes. Use a crinkle cutter or chef's knife to cut them into fries, ½ inch thick by 3 to 4 inches long.

Place the black enamel cooking pan in the bottom oven rack position to catch any drips. Place the wire metal oven rack in the second highest position.

Preheat the oven on **AIR FRY** at 400°F and set the cooking time for 13 minutes.

Place the sweet potatoes in a large mixing bowl. Drizzle the oil over the potatoes, then sprinkle on the Cajun spice blend and salt. Toss well to coat the fries evenly with the oil and seasonings. Spread out the sweet potatoes in an even layer in the air frying basket.

Air fry the sweet potatoes in the preheated oven.

When the cooking program ends, transfer the fries to serving plates. Serve right away with ketchup or sriracha mayo on the side.

Nutrition Information: Per serving: 164 calories, 2 grams fat, 33 grams carbohydrates, 5 grams fiber, 3 grams protein

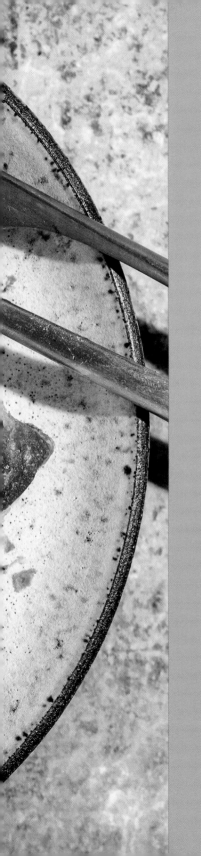

CHAPTER 8

DESSERTS

CHOCOLATE CUPCAKES with CHOCOLATE ICING

GLUTEN-FREE (use GF flour blend)

DAIRY-FREE (substitute ⅓ cup plant-based milk and 1 teaspoon apple cider vinegar for the buttermilk)

PREP TIME: 10 MINUTES, PLUS
45 MINUTES TO COOL

COOK TIME: 16 MINUTES

YIELD: 8 CUPCAKES

Moist chocolate cupcakes are complemented by an ultra-rich dark chocolate icing. If you're in need of a small batch of birthday treats whipped up in a flash, this recipe can be your new go-to. I also love baking these whenever and gifting them to neighbors in need of a treat! The icing is easy to whisk together on the stovetop, but if you're short on time, the cupcakes are also good with just a little powdered sugar on top.

CUPCAKES

¾ cup all-purpose flour

2 tablespoons Dutch-process cocoa powder

¼ teaspoon baking soda

¼ teaspoon kosher salt

½ cup granulated sugar

1 large egg

⅓ cup buttermilk

¼ cup avocado oil or other neutral-flavored oil

½ teaspoon vanilla extract

CHOCOLATE ICING

3 tablespoons unsalted butter

3 tablespoons Dutch-process cocoa powder

⅛ teaspoon kosher salt

2 tablespoons plus 1 teaspoon water

1 cup plus 2 tablespoons powdered sugar

¼ teaspoon vanilla extract

Make the cupcakes: Into a small mixing bowl, sift together the flour, cocoa powder, baking soda, and salt. In another mixing bowl, whisk together the granulated sugar and egg until evenly mixed. Whisk in the buttermilk, oil, and vanilla.

Add the dry ingredients to the wet mixture and whisk just until the flour is absorbed and the batter is smooth.

Preheat the oven on **BAKE** at 325°F and set the cooking time for 16 minutes. Place 8 silicone muffin cups on the cooking pan, and line them with paper cupcake liners. Place a cooling rack on top of a quarter sheet pan or a large dish.

Use a 3-tablespoon cookie scoop to portion the batter out into the cupcake liners, filling them about two-thirds of the way full.

Bake the cupcakes in the preheated oven.

recipe continues

When the cooking program ends, wearing heat-resistant mitts, unmold the cupcakes from the muffin cups and place them on the cooling rack. Let them cool for 30 minutes.

While the cupcakes are cooling, make the icing: In a small saucepan over medium-low heat, melt the butter. Add the cocoa powder and salt. Use a small whisk to combine until smooth. Add the water and half of the powdered sugar and whisk again until smooth. Add the remaining powdered sugar and whisk once more until the icing is once again smooth and no lumps remain. Turn off the heat. Add vanilla and whisk one last time until the vanilla is incorporated.

Spoon 1 tablespoon of the icing over each cupcake. The icing will spread out a little bit as it cools. Allow the icing to set for at least 15 minutes. Serve the cupcakes while they are still a bit warm, or let them cool to room temperature, then serve or store them in a tightly lidded container for up to 2 days.

Nutrition Information: Per cupcake with icing: 276 calories, 12 grams fat, 39 grams carbohydrates, 2 grams fiber, 2 grams protein

BASQUE-STYLE CHEESECAKE

GLUTEN-FREE (use GF flour blend)

PREP TIME: 10 MINUTES, PLUS 2 TO
24 HOURS TO COOL

COOK TIME: 33 MINUTES

YIELD: 1 (7-INCH) CHEESECAKE
(8 SERVINGS)

Unsalted butter, for greasing
the pan

1 cup heavy cream

3 large eggs

2 (8-ounce) packages cream
cheese, room temperature

¾ cup granulated sugar

2 tablespoons all-purpose
flour

¼ teaspoon kosher salt

At La Viña bar in San Sebastián, Spain, dozens of crustless, sunken-middled, nearly burnt–looking cheesecakes line the shelves. Defying all typical cheesecake logic, they are a marvel of flavor and texture. Imagine a dessert with the flavor of campfire marshmallow on the outside and a creamy, silky cheesecake filling. This mini version bakes in just 33 minutes, though you'll want to cool it completely before serving. It's traditionally enjoyed at room temperature, but it is great when chilled, too.

Generously grease a 3-inch-tall 7-inch round cake pan, then nestle a 12-inch square of parchment paper inside the pan, pleating it in a few places so that it sits as flat as possible against the sides of the pan. Use scissors to trim any excess parchment that sticks up over the sides of the pan.

In the order listed, add the cream, eggs, cream cheese, sugar, flour, and salt to a blender. Blend on medium-low speed for 20 seconds, scraping down the sides of the jar halfway through.

Preheat the oven on **BAKE** at 400°F and set the cooking time for 33 minutes.

Pour the batter into the lined pan, then place it on top of the cooking pan. Bake the cheesecake in the preheated oven.

When the cooking program ends, the cheesecake will be puffed up and deeply browned. Use an instant-read thermometer to

recipe continues

You can serve the cake at room temperature or refrigerate it and serve it chilled. You can also bake the cake up to 48 hours in advance and refrigerate until ready to serve. Bring it up to room temperature before serving, if you like.

Though it's not a traditional presentation, the sunken middle of this cheesecake begs to be filled with fresh berries in the summertime.

check the internal temperature to make sure it is at least 155°F in the center. It will still be a bit jiggly in the middle but will set up as it cools.

Wearing heat-resistant mitts, transfer the pan to a cooling rack. Let the cake cool in the pan to room temperature, about 2 hours.

Grasp an edge of the parchment to lift the cake out of the pan and onto a serving plate, with the parchment still around the cake for a rustic presentation. Cut into wedges and serve.

Nutrition Information: Per serving: 404 calories, 33 grams fat, 23 grams carbohydrates, 0 grams fiber, 6 grams protein

BUTTERMILK LIME LOAF CAKE

GLUTEN-FREE (use GF all-purpose flour blend)

DAIRY-FREE (substitute ½ cup plant-based milk and 1 teaspoon apple cider vinegar for buttermilk)

PREP TIME: 10 MINUTES, PLUS 2 HOURS AND 5 MINUTES FOR THE CAKE TO COOL AND 30 MINUTES FOR THE GLAZE TO SET

COOK TIME: 1 HOUR 5 MINUTES

YIELD: 1 LOAF CAKE (10 SERVINGS)

CAKE

1½ cups all-purpose flour, plus more for the pan

¼ teaspoon baking soda

¼ teaspoon kosher salt

1 cup granulated sugar

2 large eggs

½ cup buttermilk

½ cup avocado oil or other neutral-flavored oil, plus more for the pan

Finely grated zest of 1 lime

¼ teaspoon almond extract

¼ teaspoon vanilla extract

LIME GLAZE

1 cup powdered sugar

2 tablespoons fresh lime juice (from the zested lime)

This loaf cake is tangy from buttermilk and lime juice, with a velvety and tender crumb. Serve it for dessert with a scoop of raspberry sorbet or as an afternoon treat with coffee or tea. It keeps well on the countertop for up to 3 days, as long as it's wrapped tightly, but it probably won't last that long.

Make the cake: In a mixing bowl, sift together the flour, baking soda, and salt. In another mixing bowl, whisk together the granulated sugar and eggs for about 1 minute, until thick and pale yellow in color. Whisk in the buttermilk, oil, lime zest, and almond and vanilla extracts until the flour is absorbed.

Add the dry ingredients to the wet mixture in three batches, whisking each time until the flour is absorbed and the batter is smooth.

Preheat the oven on **BAKE** at 300°F and set the cooking time for 1 hour and 5 minutes. Grease and flour a 1½-quart Pyrex loaf pan. Place a cooling rack on top of a quarter sheet pan— this is where you will cool and glaze the cake.

Transfer the batter to the loaf pan, and place the loaf pan on top of the cooking pan. Bake the cake in the preheated oven.

When the cooking program ends, test the cake for doneness: A toothpick inserted in the middle of the cake should come out clean.

Wearing heat-resistant mitts, remove the cake from the oven and transfer the pan to the cooling rack. Let the cake cool in the pan for 5 minutes.

Run a thin spatula around the inside edges of the pan to ensure that the cake will release easily. Wearing heat-resistant mitts, carefully unmold the cake onto the cooling rack. Let the cake cool to room temperature, about 2 hours.

When the cake is fully cool, make the glaze: In a bowl, stir together the powdered sugar and lime juice until smooth. Pour the glaze all over the top of the cake, letting it drip down the sides. Let the glaze set until it is no longer shiny, about 30 minutes.

Cut the cake into approximately ¾-inch-thick slices and serve. The glazed cake will keep, unsliced and wrapped with plastic wrap or in a tightly lidded container for up to 3 days on the countertop.

Nutrition Information: Per serving: 309 calories, 12 grams fat, 47 grams carbohydrates, 1 gram fiber, 3 grams protein

JAMMY GRANOLA BARS

VEGAN (substitute vegan butter for butter)

GLUTEN-FREE (substitute GF flour blend for all-purpose flour, use GF oats)

PREP TIME: 15 MINUTES, PLUS
3 HOURS TO COOL

COOK TIME: 45 MINUTES

YIELD: 12 SQUARES

¾ cup brown sugar

¾ cup all-purpose flour

½ teaspoon kosher salt

1¼ cups old-fashioned oats

8 tablespoons unsalted butter, softened at room temperature

⅔ cup raw pecan halves, walnut halves, or whole cashews

1 cup fruit jam, any variety

These buttery, jam-filled granola bars are a versatile treat. Use any fruit jam you like for the filling, such as strawberry-rhubarb (my personal favorite), mixed berry, or apricot. Serve the bars in dessert bowls with scoops of vanilla ice cream, or pack them to take on a hike or picnic. To ensure that they hold together when slicing, allow the bars to cool for the full 3 hours recommended here.

Line an 8-inch square Pyrex baking dish with an 8×12-inch piece of parchment paper so that it goes up two sides of the dish and doesn't crimp too much in the corners.

In a food processor, combine the sugar, flour, salt, and 1 cup of the oats. Process in ten 1-second pulses until everything is finely chopped and combined.

Add 6 tablespoons of the butter to the food processor, placing it in pieces all around the food processor so it will incorporate evenly. Process in five 1-second pulses just until the butter is incorporated. Add the pecans and the remaining ¼ cup oats, and process in three 1-second pulses just until the nuts and oats are chopped and evenly distributed throughout—you should still be able to see pieces of oats and nuts.

Transfer about two-thirds of the crumb mixture from the food processor to the parchment-lined baking dish. Spread it out in an even layer, then use the bottom of a drinking glass or measuring cup to pat it down firmly.

Spoon the jam in dollops over the top of the crumb mixture layer, then use a mini offset spatula or butter knife to spread it out in an even layer. Top the jam with the remaining crumb mixture, spread it out in an even layer, then pat it down gently. Drop the remaining 2 tablespoons butter in small dabs on top of the crumb mixture.

Select **BAKE** at 325°F and set the cooking time for 45 minutes.

Place the baking dish on top of the cooking pan. Bake the bars in the preheated oven.

When the cooking program ends, remove the baking dish from the oven and allow the bars to cool completely in the pan, about 3 hours. Unmold, then slice into 12 bars. Serve right away, or store in a tightly lidded container for up to 1 week.

Nutrition Information: Per bar: 274 calories, 12 grams fat, 41 grams carbohydrates, 2 grams fiber, 2 grams protein

CHOCOLATE CHIP WALNUT OATMEAL COOKIES

VEGAN/DAIRY-FREE (substitute plant-based milk for the dairy milk and vegan butter for the butter, and use vegan chocolate chips)

GLUTEN-FREE (use GF flour blend and GF oats)

PREP TIME: 5 MINUTES, PLUS 10 MINUTES TO COOL

COOK TIME: 9 MINUTES

YIELD: 6 COOKIES

4 tablespoons unsalted butter

⅓ cup brown sugar

2 tablespoons milk (dairy or unsweetened plant-based)

½ teaspoon vanilla extract

⅔ cup all-purpose flour

½ cup old-fashioned oats

1½ teaspoons cornstarch

¼ teaspoon baking soda

¼ teaspoon kosher salt

⅓ cup chocolate chips

⅓ cup chopped walnuts

NOTES

Be sure to line the cooking pan with aluminum foil not parchment paper. It's less likely to flap around in the oven and cause the cookies to become misshapen.

This timing and temperature also works well for store-bought, preportioned cookie dough, such as the varieties from Nestle and Pillsbury. Break apart the dough into squares, roll it into balls, then bake the cookies at 325°F for 9 minutes.

When you want a few treats right away, make this small-batch recipe, which yields 6 fantastic and generously sized cookies in record time. Press them down before baking for a more traditionally shaped cookie, or leave them mounded high for ooey gooey centers. This recipe is egg-free, so you can easily make them vegan if you prefer.

In a large mixing bowl, stir together the butter, sugar, milk, and vanilla. Add the flour, oats, cornstarch, baking soda, salt, chocolate chips, and walnuts, and stir until evenly combined.

Preheat the oven on **BAKE** at 325°F and set the cooking time for 9 minutes. Line the cooking pan with aluminum foil, tucking it over the edges so it is firmly secured.

Use a 3-tablespoon cookie scoop to portion 6 cookies out onto the lined pan, about 2 inches apart. Press the cookies down a bit until they are about 2 inches in diameter. (Alternatively, you can skip the pressing step for a very domed cookie with a gooey center.)

Bake the cookies in the preheated oven.

When the cooking program ends, wearing heat-resistant mitts, remove the pan from the oven. Let the cookies cool on the pan for 10 minutes.

Use a thin flexible spatula to transfer the cookies to serving plates or a cooling rack. Serve warm or at room temperature.

Nutrition Information: Per cookie: 291 calories, 16 grams fat, 35 grams carbohydrates, 2 grams fiber, 3 grams protein

MINI PUMPKIN PIES

GLUTEN-FREE (substitute GF flour for all-purpose flour)

DAIRY-FREE (substitute coconut milk for the evaporated milk, and dairy-free whipped topping for the whipped cream)

PREP TIME: 5 MINUTES, PLUS 1 HOUR TO COOL

COOK TIME: 35 MINUTES

YIELD: 6 MINI PIES

1 (12-ounce) can evaporated milk

1 (15-ounce) can pure pumpkin puree

2 large eggs, room temperature

¾ cup brown sugar

1½ tablespoons all-purpose flour

1¼ teaspoons pumpkin pie spice

½ teaspoon kosher salt

WHIPPED CREAM

½ cup heavy cream

1 teaspoon granulated sugar

These crustless, mini pies cook and cool in about half the time of a full-size pie, so you can have delicious single-serving desserts ready to go in under 2 hours. Even better, they bake right in their serving dishes—the Corningware ramekins are so cute. Serve these at a small holiday or birthday dinner, or make them anytime.

In a blender, combine the milk, pumpkin, eggs, sugar, flour, pumpkin pie spice, and salt. Blend at medium-low speed for about 20 seconds until smooth, scraping the sides down halfway through if needed. Let the batter sit for 10 minutes, then blend once more at medium-low speed for 10 seconds.

Preheat the oven on **BAKE** at 275°F and set the cooking time for 35 minutes.

Place 6 (7-ounce) ramekins on the cooking pan. Pour the filling mixture into the ramekins, dividing it evenly between them. It should come up to the line where the lip of each ramekin begins to angle outward.

Carefully slide in the cooking pan with the ramekins and bake the mini pies in the preheated oven.

When the cooking program ends, wearing heat-resistant mitts, remove the pan of pies from the oven. Transfer the ramekins to a cooling rack, then let them cool for 1 hour. The pies will deflate slightly and come away from the sides of the ramekins as they cool.

While the pies are cooling, make the whipped cream: In a mixing bowl, combine the cream and sugar. Whisk vigorously for about 2 minutes or until soft peaks form. Cover and refrigerate until you're ready to serve.

Top each pie with a dollop of whipped cream and serve right away, or cover with plastic wrap and refrigerate for up to 2 days, then top with whipped cream just before serving.

Nutrition Information: Per mini pie with 3 tablespoons whipped cream: 323 calories, 14 grams fat, 41 grams carbohydrates, 2 grams fiber, 7 grams protein

VARIATION You can also make a full-size pumpkin pie in the air fryer oven with the classic Libby's back-of-the-can-of-pumpkin-puree recipe and a store-bought pie crust. Use the **BAKE** program at 375°F for 15 minutes, then at 325°F for an additional 40 minutes. The surface of the pie may have a slightly mottled appearance due to the convection, but it will still taste great. Nothing a dollop of whipped cream won't fix!

PUFF PASTRY APPLE TARTS

DAIRY-FREE (serve with vegan ice cream)

PREP TIME: 10 MINUTES

COOK TIME: 7 MINUTES

YIELD: 4 TARTS

1 large egg

1 tablespoon water

2 tablespoons granulated sugar

¼ teaspoon pumpkin pie spice or ground cinnamon

1 sheet store-bought frozen puff pastry, thawed for 30 minutes at room temperature until pliable but still cold

1 medium apple, quartered, cored, and sliced thinly

Vanilla ice cream, for serving (optional)

Puff pastry is incredibly easy to use. I like to use Pepperidge Farm's puff pastry, which is widely available and happens to be vegan, making these tarts dairy-free. A sheet of store-bought dough thaws on the countertop in about half an hour; then you can unfold and bake it with whatever toppings or fillings you choose. These apple tarts may just be squares of dough with an egg wash and some sliced apples on top, but they look like something you'd buy at a fancy patisserie. Serve them warm with a scoop of vanilla ice cream on top for an impressive, beautiful dessert.

In a small bowl, beat the egg and water until no streaks remain. In another small bowl, stir together the sugar and pumpkin pie spice until evenly combined.

Line the cooking pan with parchment paper.

Cut the sheet of puff pastry into 4 approximately 4-inch squares, and place them on the lined cooking pan. Use a pastry brush to coat each piece of pastry with a light layer of the egg wash.

Sprinkle 1 teaspoon of the spiced sugar onto each piece of pastry, leaving a ½-inch border of bare egg wash around the edges.

On each pastry square, arrange one-quarter of the apple slices in an overlapping pattern on top of the spiced sugar. Sprinkle ½ teaspoon of the spiced sugar on top of the apples.

recipe continues

This recipe also works well with a pear or fuyu persimmon in place of the apple.

For a glossy appearance and an extra touch of sweetness, you can brush a little bit of honey onto the apples once the tarts are baked, about 1 teaspoon per pastry.

Preheat the oven on **BAKE** at 400°F and set the cooking time for 7 minutes.

Bake the tarts in the preheated oven.

The pastry will puff up dramatically as it cooks, and the middle will deflate when it cools down after cooking. When the cooking program ends, transfer the tarts to serving plates. Serve right away with a scoop of vanilla ice cream on top, if you like.

Nutrition Information: Per serving (tart only): 286 calories, 16 grams fat, 32 grams carbohydrates, 2 grams fiber, 6 grams protein

CHOUXRROS with CHOCOLATE DIPPING SAUCE

VEGETARIAN, DAIRY-FREE
(substitute vegan butter for butter, and coconut milk for half-and-half)

PREP TIME: 15 MINUTES

COOK TIME: 7 MINUTES FOR THE DOUGH, PLUS 35 MINUTES FOR THE CHOUXRROS

YIELD: 9 CHOUXRROS AND ¾ CUP DIPPING SAUCE

CHOUXRROS

1 cup water

6 tablespoons unsalted butter

½ cup plus 2 tablespoons granulated sugar

¼ teaspoon kosher salt

1 cup all-purpose flour

3 large eggs

½ teaspoon vanilla extract

1 teaspoon ground cinnamon

CHOCOLATE DIPPING SAUCE

½ cup half-and-half

½ cup semisweet chocolate chips

Chouxrros (aka churros made with choux pastry) are not authentic to any particular cuisine, but they are delicious in their own right! The choux puffs up dramatically as it bakes in the air fryer oven, and the batons of dough come out crispy on the outside and pillowy on the inside, with a classic cinnamon sugar coating. Serve them warm with chocolate dipping sauce, or look to the pumpkin spice variation with cream cheese dip, a nod to my husband Brendan's favorite seasonal churros at Disneyland.

Make the chouxrro dough: Add the water, butter, 2 tablespoons of the sugar, and the salt to a medium saucepan over medium heat. When the butter is melted and the water is simmering, after about 4 minutes, turn the heat down to low and add the flour. Use a wooden spoon to stir vigorously for about 1 minute, until the dough has thickened and there are no lumps of flour. Continue to cook for about 3 more minutes, stirring often, until a thin film forms on the inside of the pot. Remove the pot from the heat.

Transfer the dough to a stand mixer with a paddle attachment, or a large mixing bowl. Add 1 egg and the vanilla, then beat or whisk the mixture at high speed for about 1 minute, until the egg is fully incorporated and the dough is smooth. Repeat this process with the second egg, and then the third, beating or whisking for about 1 minute after each addition, until the dough is smooth once again.

Line the cooking pan with parchment paper.

recipe continues

Insert a large star tip (Ateco 826 tip or similar) into a piping bag, then transfer the dough to the piping bag. Pipe out 9 chouxrros onto the lined cooking pan, from the top edge to the bottom edge of the pan, starting all the way over to one side. Leave about a ¾-inch space between the chouxrros.

Preheat the oven on **BAKE** at 325°F and set the cooking time for 35 minutes.

Bake the chouxrros in the preheated oven.

While the chouxrros are baking, make the chocolate sauce: Heat the half-and-half in a small saucepan over medium heat until simmering, 2 to 3 minutes. Remove the saucepan from the heat and add the chocolate chips, making sure they are fully submerged. Let sit for 1 minute, then stir vigorously for 1 to 2 minutes, until the sauce is smooth and glossy. It will be fairly liquidy at first but will thicken as it cools.

On a quarter sheet pan or a large plate, mix together the remaining sugar and the cinnamon until evenly combined.

When the cooking program ends, wearing heat-resistant mitts, remove the pan from the oven. While the chouxrros are still very hot, roll them one by one in the cinnamon sugar, using your hands to shower lots of sugar on them, making sure to sprinkle the mixture between all of the ridges. Transfer the chouxrros to serving plates and serve right away, while they're still hot, with the ramekins of chocolate sauce on the side for dipping.

VARIATION · PUMPKIN SPICE CHOUXRROS WITH CREAM CHEESE DIP Substitute pumpkin pie spice for the cinnamon in the cinnamon sugar. Instead of the chocolate sauce, make a cream cheese dip: In a bowl, stir together ½ cup room temperature cream cheese, 1 cup powdered sugar, 1 teaspoon vanilla extract, and 2 tablespoons milk.

Nutrition Information: Per serving (1 chouxrro with about 1 tablespoon chocolate sauce): 272 calories, 15 grams fat, 32 grams carbohydrates, 1 gram fiber, 4 grams protein

SLOW or FAST BROWNIES

GLUTEN-FREE (use GF flour blend)

DAIRY-FREE

PREP TIME: 10 MINUTES, PLUS
30 MINUTES TO COOL

COOK TIME: 45 MINUTES OR
2 HOURS

YIELD: 16 BROWNIES

½ cup avocado oil or other
    neutral-flavored oil, plus
    more for greasing the pan,
    or cooking spray

3 cups powdered sugar

¾ cup all-purpose flour

⅔ cup Dutch-process or natu-
    ral cocoa powder

2 large eggs

3 tablespoons water

½ teaspoon vanilla extract

¼ teaspoon kosher salt

These are classic, ultra-chocolatey brownies made with cocoa powder and other pantry ingredients you're almost sure to have on hand. Do you enjoy fudgy, dense brownies? If so, go for the longer, slower cooking time. Or for a softer, less dense brownie, choose the faster, higher temperature and baking time. Either way, you'll end up with a delicious pan of brownies, just how you like them.

Grease an 8-inch square Pyrex baking dish with oil or cooking spray.

In a large mixing bowl, sift together the sugar, flour, and cocoa. Add the ½ cup oil, the eggs, water, vanilla, and salt, and whisk until evenly combined. Pour the batter into the greased baking dish, using a spatula to spread it out in an even layer.

To slow-cook the brownies: Place the baking dish on top of the cooking pan, and place it in the oven. Select **SLOW COOK** or **BAKE** at 210°F and set the cooking time for 2 hours.

To bake the brownies faster: Preheat the oven on **BAKE** at 300°F and set the cooking time for 45 minutes. Place the baking dish on top of the cooking pan, and bake in the preheated oven.

When the cooking program ends, wearing heat-resistant mitts, remove the brownies from the oven and rest the baking dish on a cooling rack. Let the brownies cool in the pan for at least ½ hour for warm brownies or until fully cooled, about 1 hour.

Use a sharp chef's knife to cut the brownies into 16 squares, rinsing off the knife after each cut for cleaner slices. Serve warm or room temperature.

The brownies will keep, covered, on the countertop for up to 4 days or in the freezer, in a ziplock freezer bag, for up to 3 months.

Nutrition Information: Per brownie: 192 calories, 8 grams fat, 29 grams carbohydrates, 2 grams fiber, 2 grams protein

COCONUT BUTTER MOCHI

GLUTEN-FREE, DAIRY-FREE (use coconut milk and coconut oil)

PREP TIME: 5 MINUTES, PLUS
2 HOURS TO COOL
COOK TIME: 1 HOUR
YIELD: 9 LARGE SQUARES

2 large eggs

1 (13.5-ounce) can coconut milk or 1 (12-ounce) can evaporated milk

⅔ cup granulated sugar

¼ cup coconut oil or 4 tablespoons unsalted butter, melted and cooled

1⅓ cups plus 1 tablespoon (about half a box, or 8 ounces) Mochiko or Bob's Red Mill sweet rice flour

1 teaspoon baking powder

½ teaspoon coconut extract or vanilla extract

¼ teaspoon kosher salt

½ cup unsweetened shredded coconut (optional)

Additional coconut oil or butter, for greasing the pan

Butter mochi is a classic Hawaiian treat, combining flavors from Japanese and Western cuisines. Make it with dairy ingredients the traditional way, or use coconut milk and coconut oil for a tropical (and dairy-free) twist. It's delicious either way—the sweet squares are chewy in the middle and toasty and golden on the outside. Be sure to let the mochi cool for at least 2 hours before you serve it, as it becomes more and more delightfully chewy as it sits.

Add the eggs, milk, sugar, coconut oil, rice flour, baking powder, coconut extract, and salt to a blender. Blend on low speed until smooth, about 20 seconds, scraping down the sides halfway through blending. Add the shredded coconut, if you like, and blend for 2 (1-second) pulses just to combine.

Preheat the oven on **BAKE** at 300°F and set the cooking time for 1 hour. Grease an 8-inch square Pyrex baking dish lightly with butter or coconut oil.

Pour the mochi batter into the greased baking dish. Place the baking dish on the cooking pan.

Bake the mochi in the preheated oven.

When the cooking program ends, wearing heat-resistant mitts, transfer the baking dish to a cooling rack. Let the mochi cool completely in the baking dish at room temperature, about 2 hours. Unmold, cut into 9 squares, and serve right away, or store in a tightly lidded container for up to 2 days.

Nutrition Information: Per large square: 327 calories, 18 grams fat, 39 grams carbohydrates, 1 gram fiber, 4 grams protein

S'MORES

GLUTEN-FREE (use GF graham crackers)

PREP TIME: 5 MINUTES
COOK TIME: 2 MINUTES
YIELD: 4 S'MORES

4 graham cracker sheets
4 large marshmallows
1 (1.5-ounce) chocolate bar, broken into 4 sections

S'mores are such a fun and easy treat for sleepovers and movie nights, and they take minutes to make in the air fryer oven. You can make them the traditional way, or try my take on it, sandwiching the chocolate between halves of hot, toasted marshmallow for maximum meltiness. Use the classic Hershey's milk chocolate bar, or pick a dark or sea-salted bar for a more sophisticated dessert.

Preheat the oven on **BAKE** at 390°F and set the cooking time for 2 minutes for pale marshmallows or 3 minutes if you want them to get a little toasty.

Break the graham cracker sheets in half at the perforation to make 8 squares. Place them on the cooking pan. Cut the marshmallows in half, then gently push them onto the graham crackers, cut side down.

Bake the s'mores in the preheated oven.

When the cooking program ends, wearing heat-resistant mitts, remove the pan from the oven. Top half of the marshmallow-topped graham crackers with a piece of chocolate, then sandwich them with the remaining marshmallow-topped graham crackers. Let sit for a minute to allow the chocolate to melt. Serve right away.

Nutrition Information: Per s'more: 173 calories, 6 grams fat, 28 grams carbohydrates, 1 gram fiber, 2 grams protein

DRIED MINI MARSHMALLOWS and HOT COCOA MIX

GLUTEN-FREE (use GF marshmallows)

DAIRY-FREE (use any unsweetened plant-based milk to make hot cocoa)

PREP TIME: 5 MINUTES, PLUS
1 HOUR TO COOL

COOK TIME: 4 HOURS

YIELD: 2½ CUPS DEHYDRATED
MARSHMALLOWS AND
20 SERVINGS HOT COCOA MIX

2 cups mini marshmallows

HOT COCOA MIX

**1¼ cups Dutch-process or
natural cocoa powder**

2½ cups granulated sugar

1 teaspoon kosher salt

**1 teaspoon ground cinnamon
(optional)**

Dehydrating marshmallows might sound like a silly idea, but it is absolutely worth trying. They puff up as they dry, turning into adorably plump and irresistibly crunchy little sugar pillows, with a similar texture to the marshmallows in a box of Lucky Charms. Float them in a mug of hot cocoa for a festive treat. A ribbon-wrapped jar of hot cocoa mix and a cute cellophane bag of dehydrated marshmallows make a sweet homemade holiday gift.

Dehydrate the marshmallows: Spread out the marshmallows in the air frying basket in an even layer. Place the basket on the wire metal oven rack in the oven, then select **DEHYDRATE** at 150°F and set the time for 4 hours.

When the cooking program ends, wearing heat-resistant mitts, remove the basket from the oven. Let the marshmallows cool to room temperature, about 1 hour. Transfer the marshmallows to a quart-size mason jar, multiple smaller jars, or other tightly lidded container(s).

Make the hot chocolate mix: In a large mixing bowl, stir together the cocoa powder, sugar, salt, and cinnamon (if using) until evenly combined. Transfer the hot cocoa mix to a quart-size mason jar, multiple smaller jars, or other tightly lidded container(s).

The marshmallows and hot cocoa mix will keep, stored in the pantry at room temperature, for up to 6 months.

To make a serving of hot cocoa: In a mug in the microwave or in a small saucepan on the stove, heat 1 cup milk until piping hot. Stir in 3 tablespoons of the hot cocoa mix. Top the hot cocoa with mini marshmallows and serve hot.

Nutrition Information: Per serving of cocoa prepared with whole milk and topped with 8 mini marshmallows: 298 calories, 8 grams fat, 39 grams carbohydrates, 2 grams fiber, 8 grams protein

CHAPTER 9

PANTRY

SALSA RANCHERA

VEGAN, GLUTEN-FREE

PREP TIME: 5 MINUTES
COOK TIME: 10 MINUTES
YIELD: 2¼ CUPS

2 jalapeño chiles, stemmed and halved lengthwise

1 pound Roma or plum tomatoes (4 or 5 tomatoes), halved

3 cloves garlic, smashed and peeled

½ medium yellow onion, chopped

3 tablespoons fresh lime juice (from 1 lime)

¼ cup chopped fresh cilantro

1 teaspoon kosher salt

For mild salsa, remove the seeds and veins from both jalapeños. For medium salsa, leave them in one, and for hot salsa, leave them in both.

Line the cooking pan with aluminum foil. Arrange the jalapeños and tomatoes on the lined cooking pan in a single layer, cut side up. Place the pan in the oven on the highest rack position.

Select **BROIL** at 400°F and set the cooking time for 10 minutes. After 5 minutes, add the garlic cloves to the pan.

When the cooking program ends, transfer the tomatoes, jalapeños, and garlic to a blender. Add the onion, lime juice, cilantro, and salt. Process the salsa in 10 (1-second) pulses, until it is blended but still just a bit chunky. Serve the salsa right away, or transfer to a tightly lidded container and store, refrigerated, for up to 1 week.

Nutrition Information: Per serving (2 tablespoons): 9 calories, 0 grams fat, 2 grams carbohydrates, 0 grams fiber, 0 grams protein

SALSA VERDE

VEGAN, GLUTEN-FREE

PREP TIME: 5 MINUTES
COOK TIME: 10 MINUTES
YIELD: 2½ CUPS

2 jalapeño chiles, stemmed and halved lengthwise

2 Anaheim chiles, stemmed, seeded, and chopped into 2-inch pieces

½ pound tomatillos, halved, or quartered if very large

½ medium yellow onion, chopped

3 cloves garlic, smashed and peeled

3 tablespoons fresh lime juice (from 1 lime)

¼ cup chopped fresh cilantro

1½ teaspoons kosher salt

For mild salsa, remove the seeds and veins from both jalapeños. For medium salsa, leave them in one, and for hot salsa, leave them in both. Chop the jalapeños into 1-inch pieces.

Line the cooking pan with aluminum foil. Arrange the jalapeños, Anaheim chiles, tomatillos, and onion on the lined cooking pan in a single layer, cut sides up. Place the pan in the oven on the highest rack position.

Select **BROIL** and set the cooking time for 10 minutes at 400°F. After 5 minutes, add the garlic cloves to the pan.

When the cooking program ends, transfer the vegetables and any juices to a blender. Add the lime juice, cilantro, and salt. Blend at medium speed for about 30 seconds, until the salsa is fairly smooth. Serve the salsa right away, or transfer to a tightly lidded container and store, refrigerated, for up to 1 week.

Nutrition Information: Per serving (2 tablespoons): 7 calories, 0 grams fat, 1 gram carbohydrates, 0 grams fiber, 0 grams protein

LEMONY VEGAN MAYONNAISE

VEGAN, GLUTEN-FREE

PREP TIME: 5 MINUTES, PLUS
30 MINUTES TO SOAK THE
CASHEWS
YIELD: 1¼ CUPS

½ cup raw cashews

¼ cup avocado oil or other
   neutral-flavored oil

¼ cup fresh lemon juice

⅓ cup water

Finely grated zest of 1 lemon

½ teaspoon kosher salt

Add the cashews to a heat-safe bowl. Cover them with boiling water and let soak for 30 minutes.

Drain the cashews in a colander, then transfer to a blender. Add the oil, lemon juice, water, lemon zest, and salt. Blend the mixture at high speed until very smooth, with the texture of mayonnaise, about 1 minute.

Transfer the mayonnaise to a tightly lidded container and store, refrigerated, for up to 1 week. The mayonnaise will thicken a bit when chilled. It may begin to separate after a few days, but a quick stir will bring it back together.

Nutrition Information: Per tablespoon: 44 calories, 4 grams fat, 2 grams carbohydrates, 0 grams fiber, 1 gram protein

VARIATIONS · **AVOCADO CREMA** Substitute lime zest and juice for the lemon, and substitute the flesh of 1 medium avocado, cubed, for the cashews. You do not have to soak the avocado—add it straight to the blender with the other ingredients.

SRIRACHA MAYO Stir 5 tablespoons sriracha sauce into the whole batch of mayo or 1 tablespoon sriracha into ¼ cup of the mayo to make a spicy dip for sweet potato fries (page 241).

TARTAR SAUCE

VEGAN (use vegan Worcestershire)

GLUTEN-FREE (use GF Worcestershire)

PREP TIME: 5 MINUTES, PLUS 10 MINUTES TO REST

YIELD: ¾ CUP

½ cup mayonnaise (page 276)

2 tablespoons dill pickle relish or chopped pickles

2 teaspoons capers, chopped

1 tablespoon fresh lemon juice

½ teaspoon Dijon mustard

½ teaspoon Worcestershire sauce

½ teaspoon granulated sugar

¼ teaspoon dried dill

¼ teaspoon Old Bay seasoning

⅛ teaspoon ground black pepper

Stir the mayonnaise, pickle relish, capers, lemon juice, mustard, Worcestershire, sugar, dill, Old Bay, and pepper together in a small bowl. Let sit for 10 minutes, then stir once more. Serve the tartar sauce right away, or transfer it to a tightly lidded container and store, refrigerated, for up to 1 week.

Nutrition Information: Per tablespoon: 30 calories, 2 grams fat, 2 grams carbohydrates, 0 grams fiber, 1 gram protein

WHITE SHAWARMA SAUCE

GLUTEN-FREE

PREP TIME: 5 MINUTES
YIELD: 1¼ CUPS

½ cup full-fat Greek yogurt

½ cup mayonnaise (page 276)

2 cloves garlic, pressed or minced

3 tablespoons fresh lemon juice

½ teaspoon kosher salt

NOTE
For a lighter (and even tangier) sauce, you can use a higher proportion of ¾ cup Greek yogurt to ¼ cup mayonnaise.

In a small bowl, stir together the yogurt, mayonnaise, garlic, lemon juice, and salt. Serve the sauce right away, or transfer it to a tightly lidded container and store, refrigerated, for up to 1 week.

Nutrition Information: Per tablespoon: 25 calories, 2 grams fat, 2 grams carbohydrates, 0 grams fiber, 1 gram protein

ROASTED TOMATO KETCHUP

VEGAN, GLUTEN-FREE

PREP TIME: 5 MINUTES
COOK TIME: 1 HOUR 40 MINUTES
YIELD: 2 CUPS

1 pound Roma tomatoes, quartered

2 green bell peppers, stemmed, seeded, and coarsely chopped

½ medium yellow onion, coarsely chopped

2 cloves garlic, peeled

⅓ cup apple cider vinegar

⅓ cup agave nectar or honey

1 teaspoon mustard powder

½ teaspoon ground allspice

1 tablespoon kosher salt

NOTES

If you want the ketchup to be extra smooth, you can blend it once again after cooking.

For a spicy ketchup, add 2 serrano chiles, stemmed, halved, and seeded, to the blender with the rest of the ingredients.

Preheat the oven on **ROAST** at 325°F and set the cooking time for 1 hour and 40 minutes.

In a blender, combine the tomatoes, peppers, onion, garlic, vinegar, agave nectar, mustard powder, allspice, and salt in the order listed. Blend at high speed for about 1 minute, until very smooth.

Pour the blended mixture into an 8-inch square Pyrex baking dish. Place the baking dish on the cooking pan.

Roast the mixture in the preheated oven.

Every 20 minutes, wearing heat-resistant mitts, remove the baking dish from the oven. Use a wooden or silicone spoon to give the ketchup a good stir, being sure to incorporate any portions at sides of the baking dish that are cooked more. Return it to the oven.

When the cooking program ends, stir the ketchup once more. If it is thinner than you would like, cook an additional 15 minutes, then stir once more. Alternatively, if it is not as thick as you like, add 1 tablespoon water at a time, stirring it in and tasting until the ketchup has reached the desired consistency. (This can vary depending on the water content of the vegetables—you may not need to add any extra cooking time or water.)

Transfer the ketchup to a tightly lidded container and store, refrigerated, for up to 1 month.

Nutrition Information: Per tablespoon: 21 calories, 0 grams fat, 4 grams carbohydrates, 1 gram fiber, 0 grams protein

BARBECUE SAUCE

VEGAN (use agave nectar and vegan Worcestershire sauce)
GLUTEN-FREE (use GF Worcestershire sauce)

PREP TIME: 5 MINUTES
COOK TIME: 8 MINUTES
YIELD: 2 CUPS

⅔ cup ketchup (page 279)

⅓ cup apple cider vinegar

½ cup honey or agave nectar

2 tablespoons yellow mustard

1 tablespoon molasses

1 teaspoon Worcestershire sauce

1½ teaspoons seasoned salt (page 291)

½ teaspoon garlic powder

¼ teaspoon ground black pepper

⅛ teaspoon cayenne pepper (optional)

Combine the ketchup, vinegar, honey, mustard, molasses, Worcestershire, seasoned salt, garlic powder, and black pepper in a small (1½-quart) saucepan on the stove over medium heat or in an Instant Pot on its **SAUTE** program. Stir in the cayenne, if you like. Bring up to a simmer, then turn the heat down to low and simmer for 5 minutes, stirring often. Remove the pot from the heat, or turn off the Instant Pot and remove the inner pot to stop cooking the sauce.

Use the barbecue sauce right away, or transfer it to a tightly lidded container and store, refrigerated, for up to 1 month. (I actually like it best after a day or two, when the flavors have had a chance to mellow and meld.)

Nutrition Information: Per 2 tablespoons: 55 calories, 0 grams fat, 12 grams carbohydrates, 0 grams fiber, 0 grams protein

VARIATIONS For a smoky and spicy flavor, add 1 canned chipotle chile in adobo sauce, minced. For a little bit of smoky flavor without the spice, add 1 teaspoon smoked paprika.

KOREAN-STYLE DIPPING SAUCE (Ssamjang)

DAIRY-FREE

PREP TIME: 5 MINUTES
YIELD: ½ CUP

¼ cup fermented bean paste (doenjang or white miso)

2 tablespoons gochujang or sriracha sauce (see note)

1 tablespoon toasted sesame oil

2 teaspoons honey or agave nectar

1 green onion, chopped

1 clove garlic, pressed or minced

NOTE
This is a very simplified take on Korean barbecue sauce. Use doenjang for a stronger fermented bean flavor or miso for a milder sauce. Sriracha can be substituted for gochujang, but the sauce will be much spicier and won't have the same body and sweetness, so you may want to start with less sriracha and add extra honey to taste.

Combine the bean paste, gochujang, sesame oil, honey, green onion, and garlic in a small bowl. Stir until evenly mixed. Serve right away.

Nutrition Information: Per tablespoon: 45 calories, 2 grams fat, 6 grams carbohydrates, 0 grams fiber, 1 gram protein

ROASTED MARINARA SAUCE

VEGAN, GLUTEN-FREE

PREP TIME: 5 MINUTES
COOK TIME: 20 MINUTES
YIELD: 1¾ CUPS

1 pound Roma tomatoes, cut into 1-inch pieces

½ medium yellow onion, diced

2 cloves garlic, pressed or chopped

1½ tablespoons olive oil

½ teaspoon Italian seasoning

¼ teaspoon kosher salt, plus more if needed

Preheat the oven on **ROAST** at 325°F for 20 minutes. Line the cooking pan with parchment paper.

In a large mixing bowl, toss the tomatoes, onion, garlic, oil, Italian seasoning, and salt until evenly combined. Spread out the mixture on the lined cooking pan in an even layer. Roast the vegetables in the preheated oven.

When the cooking program ends, transfer the vegetables and any juices to a blender. Blend at low speed for about 30 seconds, until it is a fairly smooth sauce. Taste for seasoning, adding more salt if you like. Serve the sauce right away, or transfer it to a tightly lidded container and store, refrigerated, for up to 1 week.

Nutrition Information: Per ¼ cup: 36 calories, 2 grams fat, 4 grams carbohydrates, 1 gram fiber, 1 gram protein

VARIATION Make a quick stovetop or Instant Pot marinara sauce from canned tomatoes: In a medium saucepan over medium heat or in the Instant Pot on its **SAUTE** program, heat 1 tablespoon olive oil. Add 2 cloves garlic, pressed or minced, and sauté until bubbling and blond, about 1 minute. Add 1 teaspoon Italian seasoning and a 28-ounce can whole peeled tomatoes with their juice. Use an immersion blender to blend the sauce until smooth right in the pot. If you're going to be using the sauce in a casserole (pages 106, 147, and 185), on a pizza (page 118), or as a dipping sauce (pages 71, 72, and 94), there's no need to bring it up to a simmer or cook it further now. If you're using it as is on spaghetti or other pasta, bring up to a simmer, turn the heat down to low, and let it simmer for 10 minutes. This yields 3 cups sauce.

BURGER SAUCE

VEGAN, GLUTEN-FREE

PREP TIME: 5 MINUTES

YIELD: ⅔ CUP

1 tablespoon yellow mustard

3 tablespoons ketchup
(page 279)

4 tablespoons mayonnaise
(page 276)

½ dill pickle, minced

In a small bowl, stir together the mustard, ketchup, mayonnaise, and pickle. Use right away, or transfer it to a tightly lidded container and store, refrigerated, for up to 1 week.

Nutrition Information: Per tablespoon: 27 calories, 2 grams fat, 2 grams carbohydrates, 0 grams fiber, 0.5 gram protein

HONEY MUSTARD DIPPING SAUCE

VEGAN (use vegan mayonnaise and agave nectar)

GLUTEN-FREE

PREP TIME: 5 MINUTES

YIELD: ¾ CUP

½ cup mayonnaise (page 276)

1 tablespoon Dijon mustard

1 tablespoon whole-grain mustard

2 tablespoons clover honey or agave nectar

¼ teaspoon ground black pepper

In a small bowl, stir together the mayonnaise, mustards, honey, and pepper. Use right away, or transfer it to a tightly lidded container and store, refrigerated, for up to 1 week.

Nutrition Information: Per tablespoon: 38 calories, 2 grams fat, 3 grams carbohydrates, 0 grams fiber, 1 gram protein

SWEET CHILI GARLIC SAUCE

VEGAN, GLUTEN-FREE (substitute GF tamari for the soy sauce)

PREP TIME: 5 MINUTES
COOK TIME: 5 MINUTES
YIELD: 1⅓ CUPS

⅓ cup plus 1 tablespoon water

⅓ cup rice vinegar

⅓ cup granulated sugar

1½ tablespoons sambal oelek (chili paste)

1 tablespoon mirin (sweet cooking rice wine)

1 teaspoon soy sauce

½ teaspoon ground ginger

3 cloves garlic, pressed or minced

2 teaspoons cornstarch

In a small saucepan over medium heat, combine ⅓ cup of the water, the vinegar, sugar, sambal, mirin, soy sauce, ginger, and garlic. Stir occasionally until it comes to a simmer, about 4 minutes.

In a small bowl, stir together the cornstarch and remaining 1 tablespoon water to make a slurry. Stir it into the sauce and simmer for 1 more minute, until thickened. Let cool to room temperature before serving, or transfer to a tightly lidded container and store, refrigerated, for up to 1 month.

Nutrition Information: Per tablespoon: 19 calories, 0 grams fat, 5 grams carbohydrates, 0 grams fiber, 0 grams protein

CREAMY TAHINA

VEGAN, GLUTEN-FREE

PREP TIME: 5 MINUTES
YIELD: 1 CUP

⅓ cup water
¼ cup fresh lemon juice
⅓ cup tahini (sesame paste)
2 cloves garlic, peeled
½ teaspoon kosher salt
⅛ teaspoon ground cumin

Add the water, lemon juice, tahini, garlic, salt, and cumin to a blender in the order listed. Blend at medium speed for about 1 minute, until smooth. Taste for seasoning, adding more salt if needed. Serve right away, or transfer to a tightly lidded container and store, refrigerated, for up to 1 week. It may begin to separate after a few days, but a quick stir will bring it back together.

Nutrition Information: Per 2 tablespoons: 64 calories, 6 grams fat, 2 grams carbohydrates, 1 gram fiber, 2 grams protein

CASHEW GARLIC and HERB CREAM CHEESE

VEGAN, GLUTEN-FREE

PREP TIME: 5 MINUTES, PLUS
30 MINUTES TO SOAK THE
CASHEWS

YIELD: 1 CUP

½ cup raw cashews

¼ cup avocado oil or other
   neutral-flavored oil

2 tablespoons water

2 tablespoons fresh lemon
   juice

½ teaspoon Italian seasoning

½ teaspoon kosher salt

¼ teaspoon garlic powder

NOTE
For a plain, neutral-flavored
vegan cream cheese, omit the
Italian seasoning and garlic
powder.

Add the cashews to a heat-safe bowl. Cover them with boiling water and let soak for 30 minutes.

Drain the cashews in a colander, then transfer to a blender. Add the oil, water, lemon juice, Italian seasoning, salt, and garlic powder. Blend the mixture at high speed until very smooth, about 1 minute.

Use the cream cheese right away, or transfer it to a tightly lidded container and store, refrigerated, for up to 1 week.

Nutrition Information: Per serving (2 tablespoons): 101 calories, 10 grams fat, 2 grams carbohydrates, 0 grams fiber, 1 gram protein

BARBECUE RUB

VEGAN, GLUTEN-FREE

PREP TIME: 5 MINUTES
YIELD: 1 CUP

½ cup brown sugar
2 tablespoons chili powder
1 tablespoon smoked paprika
2 teaspoons ground cumin
2 teaspoons dried thyme
2 teaspoons mustard powder
2 teaspoons kosher salt
1 teaspoon garlic powder
1 teaspoon onion powder
1 teaspoon dried oregano
1 teaspoon ground black
    pepper

In a bowl, stir together the sugar, chili powder, paprika, cumin, thyme, mustard, salt, garlic powder, onion powder, oregano, and pepper until evenly combined. Use right away, or transfer to a tightly lidded container and store in the pantry for up to 1 year.

Nutrition Information: Per tablespoon: 32 calories, 0 grams fat, 8 grams carbohydrates, 0.5 gram fiber, 0.5 gram protein

POULTRY SEASONING

VEGAN, GLUTEN-FREE

PREP TIME: 5 MINUTES
YIELD: ½ CUP

3 tablespoons dried sage
3 tablespoons dried thyme
1 tablespoon dried oregano
1 teaspoon dried rosemary
1 teaspoon ground ginger
1 teaspoon ground black
    pepper

Combine the sage, thyme, oregano, rosemary, ginger, and pepper in a spice grinder or mortar and pestle. Grind until mostly smooth. (Alternatively, if you are using all ground rather than whole or crumbled herbs, you can mix them together in a small bowl.) Use right away, or transfer to a tightly lidded container and store in the pantry for up to 1 year.

Nutrition Information: Per ¼ teaspoon: 0 calories, 0 grams fat, 0 grams carbohydrates, 0 grams fiber, 0 grams protein

SHAWARMA SPICE BLEND

VEGAN, GLUTEN-FREE

PREP TIME: 5 MINUTES
YIELD: ¼ CUP

1 tablespoon ground coriander
1 tablespoon kosher salt
1 teaspoon ground black
    pepper
1 teaspoon ground cinnamon
1 teaspoon ground cumin
1 teaspoon ground turmeric
1 teaspoon ground ginger
¼ teaspoon ground cloves

NOTE
Use 1 tablespoon per pound of
boneless chicken (page 175) or
lamb.

In a small bowl, stir together the coriander, salt, pepper, cinnamon, cumin, turmeric, ginger, and cloves until evenly combined. Use right away, or transfer to a tightly lidded container and store in the pantry for up to 1 year.

Nutrition Information: Per ¾ teaspoon: 3 calories, 0 grams fat, 1 gram carbohydrates, 0 grams fiber, 0 grams protein

SEASONED SALT

VEGAN, GLUTEN-FREE

PREP TIME: 5 MINUTES
YIELD: ⅓ CUP

¼ cup fine sea salt

1 teaspoon granulated sugar

1 teaspoon ground black pepper

1 teaspoon sweet paprika

½ teaspoon garlic powder

½ teaspoon onion powder

¼ teaspoon ground turmeric

¼ teaspoon cayenne pepper

In a small bowl, stir together the salt, sugar, black pepper, paprika, garlic powder, onion powder, turmeric, and cayenne until evenly combined. Use right away, or transfer to a tightly lidded container and store in the pantry for up to 1 year.

Nutrition Information: Per ¼ teaspoon: 0 calories, 0 grams fat, 0 grams carbohydrates, 0 grams fiber, 0 grams protein

YEASTED YOGURT FLATBREADS

VEGETARIAN

PREP TIME: 20 MINUTES, PLUS
1 HOUR TO PROOF

COOK TIME: 20 MINUTES

YIELD: 8 FLATBREADS

2 cups bread flour

½ cup whole-wheat flour

1½ teaspoons instant yeast

1½ teaspoons kosher salt

2 teaspoons granulated sugar

½ cup warm water (110°F to 115°F)

⅔ cup full-fat or low-fat Greek yogurt

2 tablespoons olive oil, plus more for rolling

Za'atar seasoning or sesame seeds, for sprinkling (optional)

Combine the bread flour, whole-wheat flour, yeast, salt, sugar, water, yogurt, and oil in a bowl of a stand mixer. Knead with a dough hook for 6 minutes, until it is a stretchy, sticky ball with well-formed strands of gluten. (You can also do this in a mixing bowl with a dough whisk.)

Transfer the dough to a bowl that fits in your oven (check to be sure). Cover the bowl with a reusable silicone lid or other sturdy cover that won't blow off the bowl when the air fryer fan is on. (You don't want to use plastic wrap for this, as it's likely to come off.)

Select **PROOF** or **DEHYDRATE** at 100°F and set the time for 1 hour. Place the bowl in the oven.

When the cooking program ends, the dough should have doubled in size. Remove the bowl from the oven. Lightly oil a work surface. Divide the dough into 8 equal pieces and roll each into a ball. Use a lightly oiled rolling pin to roll out each ball into a 6-inch circle.

Preheat the oven on **BAKE** at 400°F and set the cooking time for 20 minutes. Line a quarter sheet pan with parchment paper.

Place 2 of the flatbreads on the lined quarter sheet pan. Place the quarter sheet pan on top of the cooking pan. If you like, sprinkle the flatbreads with za'atar or sesame seeds.

Bake the flatbreads in the preheated oven for 5 minutes. The flatbreads should be baked through, puffed up, and beginning to brown. Wearing heat-resistant mitts, remove the pan from the

For larger flatbreads, divide the dough into 4 balls rather than 8, roll them out into 8×7-inch rectangles, and bake them one at a time.

oven and transfer the flatbreads to a cooling rack. Repeat with remaining flatbreads, two at a time—you can put the next batch right on the hot quarter sheet pan, reusing the parchment, or have a second lined pan ready to go.

Serve the flatbreads right away, or let cool to room temperature, then store in a tightly lidded container or ziplock bag for up to 3 days at room temperature or up to 1 month in the freezer.

Nutrition Information: Per flatbread: 192 calories, 5 grams fat, 29 grams carbohydrates, 2 grams fiber, 6 grams protein

VARIATION · GARLIC NAAN Instead of rounds, shape the dough into ovals about 8 inches long and 5 inches wide. In a small bowl, stir together 2 tablespoons melted butter, 2 cloves garlic, pressed or minced, and 1 teaspoon chopped fresh cilantro or parsley. Right after each bread comes out of the oven, brush the top with some of the mixture.

PORK RIND BREADING

GLUTEN-FREE, DAIRY-FREE

PREP TIME: 10 MINUTES
YIELD: 3⅓ CUPS

1 (5-ounce) bag plain pork
  rinds or chicharrones
1¼ cups blanched almond flour
1 tablespoon sweet paprika
1½ teaspoons garlic powder
1½ teaspoons dried oregano
1 teaspoon ground black
  pepper
1 teaspoon kosher salt
½ teaspoon cayenne pepper

NOTE
Use this breading on pork
chops (page 161) or chicken
tenders (page 179) for a flavorful, low-carb alternative to
grain-based breading.

In a food processor, process the pork rinds in about 20 (1-second) pulses, until they form a fairly smooth powder but have not begun to get oily or clump together. You may need to work in batches, depending on the size of your food processor—it will process the pork rinds best if it is about halfway full.

Transfer the pork rinds to a mixing bowl and add the almond flour, paprika, garlic powder, oregano, black pepper, salt, and cayenne. Stir until evenly combined.

Use the breading right away, or transfer to a 1-quart ziplock freezer bag or tightly lidded container and store, refrigerated, for up to 2 weeks or frozen for up to 3 months.

Nutrition Information: Per 2 tablespoons: 87 calories, 6 grams fat, 2 grams carbohydrates, 1 gram fiber, 6 grams protein

REFRIGERATOR PIZZA DOUGH

VEGAN, DAIRY-FREE

PREP TIME: 5 MINUTES, PLUS
40 MINUTES TO PROOF

YIELD: ABOUT 1 POUND DOUGH,
ENOUGH FOR 2 MEDIUM (12-INCH)
PIZZAS

3¾ cups bread flour or all-purpose flour

1½ teaspoons kosher salt

2 teaspoons instant yeast

1¼ cups plus 2 tablespoons and 2 teaspoons warm water (110°F to 115°F)

NOTE

Using warm water is critical to the fast proofing time of this dough. If you use colder water, it will take much longer to double in size. Just be sure the water is not too hot—at temperatures above 120°F, the yeast will begin to die off, and the dough will not rise as well.

This recipe makes enough dough for 2 medium pizzas, and it keeps in the fridge for up to 1 week, so you can use some right away and also have pizza again whenever the mood strikes. The dough proofs in the air fryer oven on its **PROOF** or **DEHYDRATE** program—use whichever you have on your machine. The odd amount of water is on purpose—this proportion of flour to water makes a 75% hydration dough, ideal for a chewy pizza crust.

In a bowl that will fit in your oven (check to be sure), stir together the flour, salt, and yeast. Pour in the water, then use a dough whisk or wooden spoon to combine the ingredients into a shaggy dough. Knead the dough with the whisk for about 2 minutes, until it is starting to become stretchy and comes away from the bowl. It will still be very sticky.

Cover the bowl with a reusable silicone lid or other sturdy cover that won't blow off the bowl when the air fryer fan is on. (You don't want to use plastic wrap for this, as it's likely to come off.) Place the covered bowl in the oven. Select **PROOF** or **DEHYDRATE** at 95°F and set the time for 40 minutes.

When the cooking program ends, the dough should have doubled in size. Use the dough right away, or transfer it to a tightly lidded container or 1-gallon ziplock bag and store in the refrigerator for up to 1 week. The dough may expand during storage; open the container to let out the excess air periodically if needed.

Nutrition Information: Per 1/16 of the recipe (1 slice of pizza's worth of dough): 105 calories, 0 grams fat, 21 grams carbohydrates, 1 gram fiber, 4 grams protein

BREAD CRUMBS

Varies depending on the variety of bread used

PREP TIME: 5 MINUTES, PLUS
30 MINUTES TO COOL
COOK TIME: 2 TO 3 HOURS
YIELD: ABOUT 2 CUPS

6 slices bread (about
   12 ounces), cut into
   ½-inch cubes

Make your own custom bread crumbs at home, and the options are endless. You can use slices of whatever bread you like, such as tangy sourdough, whole-grain, or even a gluten-free loaf. I hardly ever buy a canister of bread crumbs anymore since these are so easy to make.

Arrange the cubed bread in the air frying basket in an even layer. Place the basket on the wire oven rack in the oven. Select **DEHYDRATE** at 130°F and set the time for 2 hours.

When the cooking program ends, check to make sure that the bread is completely dry and crisp (this can vary based on the variety of bread used). If any pieces feel at all soft, select **DEHYDRATE** and set the time for an additional hour at 130°F.

Wearing heat-resistant mitts, remove the basket from the oven. Let the bread cool completely, about 30 minutes.

Transfer the bread to a food processor and process in 1-second pulses until you have fine, evenly processed bread crumbs. Transfer to a tightly lidded container and store in a cool, dry place for up to 1 month.

Nutrition Information: Per ¼ cup: 100 calories, 1 gram fat, 18 grams carbohydrates, 2 grams fiber, 4 grams protein

VARIATION · ITALIAN BREAD CRUMBS Add 1 teaspoon Italian seasoning, ½ teaspoon garlic powder, and ½ teaspoon salt.

CROUTONS

VEGAN (substitute vegan butter for the butter)
GLUTEN-FREE (use GF bread)

PREP TIME: 10 MINUTES
COOK TIME: 10 MINUTES
YIELD: 4 CUPS

4 slices sourdough or French bread (8 ounces total)

2 tablespoons unsalted butter, melted

2 tablespoons olive oil

2 cloves garlic, pressed or minced

2 tablespoons chopped fresh parsley

½ teaspoon seasoned salt (page 291)

Cut the bread into ½- to ¾-inch cubes, as large as you like your croutons. Place the cubed bread in a large mixing bowl.

Preheat the oven on **BAKE** at 350°F and set the cooking time for 10 minutes. Line the cooking pan with parchment paper or aluminum foil.

In a small bowl, stir together the butter, oil, garlic, parsley, and seasoned salt. Drizzle the butter mixture over the cubed bread and toss to combine. Spread out the croutons on the lined cooking pan in a single layer.

Bake the croutons in the preheated oven. When the "**turn food**" message comes on, give them a stir, then return them to the oven.

When the cooking program ends, remove the croutons from the oven. Use the croutons right away, or let them cool to room temperature, about 20 minutes. Store in a tightly lidded container or ziplock bag for up to 1 week.

Nutrition Information: Per ¼ cup: 60 calories, 3 grams fat, 6 grams carbohydrates, 0 grams fiber, 1 gram protein

Time and Temperature Chart for Fresh and Frozen Foods

FOOD	SMART PROGRAM	COOKING TEMPERATURE	COOKING TIME	ACCESSORY	RACK POSITION AND NOTES
Asparagus	**AIR FRY**	400°F/205°C	4 minutes	Cooking pan	Middle position; turn partway
Beef jerky	**DEHYDRATE**	135°F/57°C	4 to 5 hours	Air frying basket on oven rack	Middle or highest position; set it and forget it
Beef steak	**AIR FRY**	400°F/205°C	13 to 15 minutes	Cooking pan	Middle position; turn partway
Cake	**BAKE**	355°F/179°C	30 minutes	Cake pan or baking dish on cooking pan	Lowest position; set it and forget it
Cauliflower florets	**AIR FRY**	350°F/177°C	10 to 15 minutes	Cooking pan	Middle position; turn partway
Corn, on the cob	**ROAST**	450°F/232°C	7 minutes	Cooking pan or air frying basket on oven rack	Middle position; turn partway
Corn dogs	**AIR FRY**	400°F/205°C	15 minutes	Air frying basket on oven rack	Middle position; turn partway
Chicken, rotisserie style	**ROAST**	380°F/193°C	45 minutes	Rotisserie spit	Set it and forget it
Chicken, quartered	**ROAST**	400°F/205°C	18 minutes	Cooking pan	Middle position; turn partway
Chicken nuggets, frozen	**BROIL**	400°F/205°C	10 minutes	Cooking pan	Middle position; turn partway
Chicken wings, fresh	**AIR FRY**	400°F/205°C	10 to 12 minutes	Cooking pan or air frying basket on oven rack	Middle position; turn partway
Chicken wings, frozen	**AIR FRY**	400°F/205°C	12 minutes	Cooking pan or air frying basket on oven rack	Middle position; turn partway
Cupcakes	**BAKE**	365°F/187°C	13 to 14 minutes	Silicone muffin cups on cooking pan	Lowest position; set it and forget it
Eggs, large, in shell	**AIR FRY**	250°F/121°C	15 or 20 minutes (soft or hard boiled)	Air frying basket on oven rack	Middle position; set it and forget it
Falafel, frozen	**AIR FRY**	400°F/205°C	7 to 10 minutes	Cooking pan	Middle position; turn partway
Fish sticks, frozen	**BROIL**	400°F/205°C	10 to 12 minutes	Air frying basket on oven rack	Middle position; turn partway
Fries, fresh	**AIR FRY**	400°F/205°C	22 to 25 minutes	Air frying basket on oven rack	Middle position; shake partway

FOOD	SMART PROGRAM	COOKING TEMPERATURE	COOKING TIME	ACCESSORY	RACK POSITION AND NOTES
Fries, frozen	AIR FRY	400°F/205°C	12 to 15 minutes	Air frying basket on oven rack	Middle position; shake partway
Fruit leather	DEHYDRATE	135°F to 150°F/57°C to 66°C	6 to 8 hours	Cooking pan or air frying basket on oven rack	Middle or highest position; turn partway
Hash browns, frozen (patties or shredded)	AIR FRY	400°F/205°C	10 minutes	Air frying basket on oven rack	Middle position; turn partway
Hot dogs	AIR FRY	400°F/205°C	7 to 9 minutes	Air frying basket on oven rack	Middle position; set it and forget it
Mozzarella sticks, frozen	AIR FRY	360°F/185°C	6 minutes	Air frying basket on oven rack	Middle position; turn partway
Muffins	BAKE	350°F/177°C	15 minutes	Silicone muffin cups on cooking pan	Lowest position; set it and forget it
Nachos	BROIL	400°F/205°C	4 minutes	Cooking pan	Middle position
Pizza, frozen (thin crust)	BAKE	400°F/205°C	8 to 10 minutes	Cooking pan	Lowest position; set it and forget it
Potato or veggie tots, frozen	AIR FRY	400°F/205°C	8 to 10 minutes	Air frying basket on oven rack	Middle position; shake partway
Salmon, fresh	BROIL	400°F/205°C	8 to 10 minutes	Cooking pan	Middle or highest position; set it and forget it
Shrimp, fresh	AIR FRY	400°F/205°C	3 to 5 minutes	Cooking pan or air frying basket on oven rack	Middle position; turn partway
Shrimp, frozen	AIR FRY	380°F/193°C	4 to 6 minutes	Cooking pan or air frying basket on oven rack	Middle position; turn partway
Spanakopita, frozen	BAKE	320°F/160°C	10 minutes	Cooking pan	Middle position; turn partway
Taquitos	AIR FRY	400°F/205°C	10 minutes	Air frying basket on oven rack	Middle position; turn partway
Veggie burgers, frozen	AIR FRY	400°F/205°C	12 to 15 minutes	Air frying basket on oven rack	Middle position; turn partway
Waffles, frozen	TOAST	Select # of waffles	Toast Level 2	Oven rack	Middle position
White fish fillet, fresh	BROIL	400°F/205°C	3 to 4 minutes	Cooking pan	Middle or top position; set it and forget it

Cooking times are a recommendation only. Always use a meat thermometer to ensure the internal temperature reaches a safe minimum temperature. Refer to the USDA's Safe Minimum Internal Temperature Chart for more information, available online at https://www.fsis.usda.gov

ACKNOWLEDGMENTS

What a fun project this has been, writing a cookbook full of crispy roasted, baked, and browned foods for this fabulous and futuristic appliance, the air fryer oven. I am grateful to so many people for supporting me and helping me to make it happen.

To my husband, every day working from home with you has been a blessing, even in a year when we saw more of each other than we previously could have thought possible. Thank you so much for your love and support. It's only because of our strong partnership that I'm able to do what I do.

To my daughter, Eve, you are the brightest light and my biggest joy. You've been there for the development of virtually every recipe in this book, whether hanging out in your discovery tower at kitchen counter level or sitting on the floor rearranging the cupboards. Thank you for your company, your sweetness, and your patience.

To my agent, Alison Fargis, thank you for your endless support and for helping me to find a publisher for this book.

To the team at HarperCollins, thank you for working with me to make this cookbook. Thanks to editor Karen Murgolo and her incredible assistant, Jacqueline Quirk, copy editor Suzanne Fass, art director Melissa Lotfy, photographer Katie Newburn, and food stylist Nathan Carrabba for your time, talent, and hard work in helping to bring everything together and make this book so beautiful. Thank you also to the marketing team at HarperCollins, including Andrea DeWerd, Katie Tull, and Matt Schweitzer, and to my publicist, Bridget Nocera, as well as the wonderful sales force for your support and enthusiasm.

To Mary Roy, Justin Lim, Zachary MacLeod, and the rest of the team at Instant Brands, thank you for supporting me in the writing of my sixth authorized cookbook. I'm always excited to see what incredible kitchen technology you produce, and it's so much fun to write recipes that make use of it.

To my recipe testers, Heather Nelson, Larry and Cindy Harris, and Ashley Powell, thank you for your careful testing and detailed feedback. It's one thing to follow a recipe, but it's another to help someone write one.

And finally, thank you to all of the air fryer oven enthusiasts I have met and interacted with along the way. Your eagerness to cook with your appliances is a big reason for why I write my cookbooks. I couldn't be happier to help you make the most of your kitchen gadgets and gizmos.

INDEX

Note: Page references in *italics* indicate photographs.